Second Edition

HANDBOOK for

CITIZENSHIP

MARGARET SEELY

PRENTICE HALL REGENTS
Upper Saddle River, New Jersey 07458

This book is dedicated to my husband,
Contee Seely. Without his support, hard work,
and constant encouragement there would
have been no book.

Project Editor: Helen Munch
Copyeditor: Marc Lecard
Production/Design: E. Carol Gee
Cover Illustration: C. Buck Reynolds
Composition: Arlene Hardwick, Elizabeth Tong

 © 1989 by Prentice Hall Regents
Prentice-Hall, Inc.
Simon & Schuster / A Viacom Company
Upper Saddle River, New Jersey 07458

Printed in the United States of America

10

ISBN   0-13-372806-4

Prentice-Hall International (UK) *Limited, London*
Prentice-Hall of Australia Pty. *Limited, Sydney*
Prentice-Hall Canada Inc., *Toronto*
Prentice-Hall Hispanoamericana, S.A., *Mexico*
Prentice-Hall of India Private Limited, *New Delhi*
Prentice-Hall of Japan, Inc., *Tokyo*
Simon & Schuster Asia Pte. Ltd., *Singapore*
Editora Prentice-Hall do Brasil, Ltda., *Rio de Janeiro*

TABLE OF CONTENTS

Foreword

My original purpose in writing *Handbook for Citizenship* was to provide a simple, comprehensive guide for those people studying for the U.S. naturalization examination. Since the exam is almost entirely oral, a written guide can be a helpful tool.

In the *Handbook*'s first edition, I attempted to indicate the bare minimum of information likely to be covered in the average exam. At the same time, I provided additional background and detail for those interested. I also emphasized the basic vocabulary needed by most candidates for the exam.

In this second edition of *Handbook for Citizenship*, I have tried to improve both the quality and quantity of the original material and to meet the needs of students and teachers throughout the United States. I have also stressed the <u>oral</u> use of the book both in the To the Student notes that follow and in the accompanying *Teacher's Manual.* New to the second edition are the *Teacher's Manual* itself, small facsimiles of the naturalization petition forms, an Answer Key for the B and C exercises, and extensive information on the 50 states (see Appendices). A final addition is a special audio cassette tape (Note the ordering information above for p. 2.) with sample Practice Questions and Answers from previous naturalization exams.

The class in which these materials were developed over the years has included a wide variety of people: those who barely wrote, read, understood or spoke English and those whose native language was English; those who had never attended school and those who had been university professors in their own countries; those who just wanted to memorize the minimum number of English questions and answers for the exam and those who wanted to learn about U.S. history and government; those who especially wanted to learn more English while preparing for the exam; people between the ages of 18 and 90 and people from at least 50 countries who spoke almost as many languages.

The changes and improvements in *Handbook for Citizenship, Second Edition* make it a better tool for those undertaking the process of becoming a U.S. citizen. Now the book can be used both by teachers and students in the classroom and by students working at home. I hope it will also simplify the task of learning about and becoming a U.S. citizen for everyone.

Margaret Seely

Margaret Seely
September, 1988

U.S. Map with State Lines

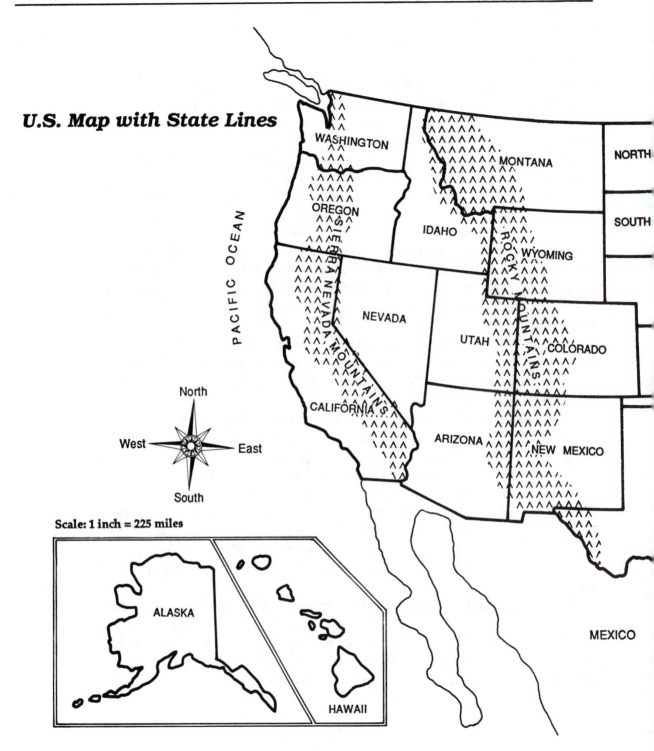

PACIFIC OCEAN

WASHINGTON

OREGON

SIERRA NEVADA MOUNTAINS

NEVADA

CALIFORNIA

North

West · East

South

Scale: 1 inch = 225 miles

ALASKA

HAWAII

MONTANA

IDAHO

WYOMING

ROCKY MOUNTAINS

UTAH

COLORADO

ARIZONA

NEW MEXICO

NORTH

SOUTH

MEXICO

CANADA

DAKOTA
MINNESOTA
WISCONSIN
DAKOTA
MICHIGAN
Mississippi River
NEBRASKA
IOWA
ILLINOIS
INDIANA
OHIO
KANSAS
MISSOURI
KENTUCKY
TENNESSEE
OKLAHOMA
ARKANSAS
TEXAS
ALABAMA
LOUISIANA
MISSISSIPPI
FLORIDA

MAINE
VERMONT
NEW HAMPSHIRE
MASSACHUSETTS
NEW YORK
RHODE ISLAND
CONNECTICUT
NEW JERSEY
DELAWARE
PENNSYLVANIA
MARYLAND
WEST VIRGINIA
Washington, D.C.
VIRGINIA
NORTH CAROLINA
SOUTH CAROLINA
GEORGIA

ATLANTIC OCEAN

GULF OF MEXICO

CUBA

indicates the area of
the first 13 states—
with present borders.

To the Student

The naturalization exam is almost entirely oral and *Handbook for Citizenship, Second Edition* is intended for oral use.

To study with this book:
- read the lessons and exercises <u>aloud</u>.
- listen and respond orally to someone else reading the material aloud.
- talk about the material with another person.
- <u>do not write</u> answers to the exercise questions in the book. (The naturalization exam is oral, and you need to be able to use the exercises for review. You cannot check how well you remember the answers if they are written in the book.)
- note the following in the exercises:
  - plurals, past tenses and related forms of words are provided in the word lists
  - the same questions are repeated on purpose for emphasis in a single lesson and throughout the book
  - two questions in an exercise may have the same answer.
- pay special attention to important items marked like this ➡.
- review the Practice Questions on pp. 98–103 by covering up the answers.
- review the Practice Questions by listening and responding to the tape (available for separate purchase from Alemany Press).
- practice writing the sentences on p. 104. Fill in the blanks and be sure you can spell the words correctly. (You will be asked to write a simple English sentence during your naturalization exam.)

To use the charts and appendices effectively:
- fill in the names of your U.S. government officers on the Government Officers Chart, p. 61.
- fill in the information about your state, county and city officers on the State and Local Government Officers Chart, p. 71.
- ask your teacher (or local public librarian) to help you find information you cannot find yourself.
- read and learn about your state in "The 50 States," pp. 74–82.
- refer to the material on California, Alameda County, and the city of Oakland on pp. 83–89 as examples of the information you need about your state and local governments. Be sure you can answer the questions in the "State and Local Government" lessons.

HAPPY LEARNING and GOOD LUCK!

NATURALIZATION

Filing for Naturalization

Who May File?

You may file an application, a "Petition for Naturalization," to become a U.S. citizen when you have been a U.S. resident with an alien registration card for at least five years. You must also have met the other requirements for citizenship listed in the booklet *Naturalization Requirements and General Information Form N-17*, available from the Immigration and Naturalization Service (INS). However, a registered alien is <u>never</u> required to become a citizen.

What Do You Need?

To apply for citizenship you will need:

- Application to File/Petition for Naturalization, Form N-400*
- Fingerprint cards
- Three 2" x 2" (passport size) photographs of yourself taken within 30 days.

You can pick up the forms and fingerprint cards at the INS office nearest you. Look in the phone book under " U.S. Government, Justice Department."

What Do You Do?

Fill out the forms completely and have your fingerprints taken at the nearest police station (usually for a fee) or at INS offices (after a very long wait). <u>Photocopy</u> your completed forms for yourself.

Find out where to send the completed forms, fingerprint cards, and pictures. Then send them by registered mail. You must also send a money order for $95.00. You can also deliver them in person, but it's not a good idea. You will probably wait from four to eight months before you are notified by mail to appear for your examination.

---

*Copies of these forms appear on pp. 13–17 in a reduced size.

Preparing For and Taking the Examination

It is a good idea to review the questions and answers on the petition forms before you take your exam. If you do not pass the exam the first time, you may take it two more times. After that, you must send in new papers.

At the beginning of your examination, the examiner will ask you to raise your right hand and swear to tell the truth. Then you will be asked several questions from your petition forms. Some examiners next ask about history and government. Others mix up the questions. Listen carefully and be sure you <u>never</u> answer a question you don't understand. It's all right to say, "I don't understand," or "Please repeat that." You will <u>not</u> fail the examination if you do so. The examiner will ask you to write a simple sentence in English.

If you pass the examination, you will receive a receipt for passing the examination. <u>Be sure to keep this receipt</u>. After another three or four months, the INS will notify you when you are to appear in court to take the oath of citizenship. At that time you will give up your alien registration card ("green card") and receive your citizenship papers. Then you will be a citizen of the United States. Congratulations!

Rights and Responsibilities of U.S. Citizenship

Rights

As a U.S. citizen you have the following rights:

- to vote
- to hold a government job
- to have a U.S. passport
- to be elected to a government position
- to sit on a jury
- <u>not</u> to be sent out of the U.S.

Responsibilities

Some rights are also responsibilities (jobs or duties). The United States is a government of the people. That is, the people control the government. The government does not work well if the people do not take part. Therefore, as a citizen you also have these responsibilities:

- to vote
- to sit on a jury
- to follow the laws
- to try to change bad laws
- to respect the rights of others
- to teach your children the rights and ideas that are important in this country

THESE FORMS ARE OBSOLETE. YOU CAN GET THE CORRECT FORMS AT YOUR NEAREST NATURALIZATION OFFICE

U.S. Department of Justice
Immigration and Naturalization Service

Application to File   OMB #1115-0009
Petition for Naturalization

Please read the instructions before filling out this form.

This block for government use only.
Section of Law

1. Your name (Exactly as it appears on your Alien Registration Receipt Card)

2. Your Alien Registration number   3. Your Social Security Number
A-

4. Your name (Full true and correct name, if different from above)

5. Any other names you have used (Including maiden)

6. Your date of birth (Month/Day/Year)   7. Your Sex
☐ Male   ☐ Female

8. Your place of birth (City or Town)

(County, Province or State)   (Country)

9. Was your father or mother ever a United States citizen?
(If Yes, explain fully)   ☐ Yes   ☐ No

10. Can you read and write English?
☐ Yes   ☐ No

11. Can you speak English?
☐ Yes   ☐ No

12. Can you sign your name in English?
☐ Yes   ☐ No

13. Date you were admitted for permanent residency (Month/Day/Year)

14. Place you were admitted for permanent residency (City and State)

15. Date your continuous residency began in the U.S. (Month/Day/Year)

16. How long have you continuously resided in the State where you now live?
(Number of Months)

17. Do you intend to reside permanently in the United States?
(If No, explain fully)   ☐ Yes   ☐ No

18. Have you served in the United States Armed Forces?
(If Yes, complete all of #18.)   ☐ Yes   ☐ No
Branch of Service (Indicate if Reserve or National Guard)
☐ Inducted   ☐ Enlisted
Location where you entered (City and State)

Service began (Month/Day/Year)

Service ended (Month/Day/Year)

Service number

Rank at discharge

Type of discharge (Honorable, Dishonorable, etc.)

Reason for discharge (Alienage, conscientious objector, other)

19. At what addresses in the United States have you lived during the last 5 years? List present address *first.*

Street Address	City *county* and State	From (Month/Day/Year)	To (Month/Day/Year)
			Present

20. What employment have you held during the last 5 years? List present or most recent employment *first.* (If none, write "None".)

Name and Address of Employer	Occupation or Type of Business	From (Month/Day/Year)	To (Month/Day/Year)

Form N-400 (12/05/86) N

21. What is your present marital status?

☐ Married   ☐ Widowed   ☐ Divorced   ☐ Single

22. Complete the following *regarding your husband or wife if you are currently married.*

First (given) name	Date married (Month/Day/Year)	Date of birth (Month/Day/Year)	Country of birth
Place he or she entered the U.S.	Date entered the U.S. (Month/Day/Year)	His or her Alien Registration Number	Present immigration status
Date naturalized (Month/Day/Year)	Place naturalized	Present address (street and number)	City and State or country

23. Complete the following if you were previously married.   Total number of times you have been married. _____

Name of prior husband or wife	Date of marriage (Month/Day/Year)	Date marriage ended (Month/Day/Year)	How marriage ended	INS status
				☐ Alien ☐ Citizen
				☐ Alien ☐ Citizen
				☐ Alien ☐ Citizen

24. Complete the following if your present husband or wife was previously married.   Total number of times your husband or wife has been married. _____

Name of prior husband or wife	Date of marriage (Month/Day/Year)	Date marriage ended (Month/Day/Year)	How marriage ended	INS status
				☐ Alien ☐ Citizen
				☐ Alien ☐ Citizen
				☐ Alien ☐ Citizen

25. Complete all columns for each of your children. (If child lives with you, state "with me" in Location column; otherwise, give the City and State of that child's residence.)   Indicate your total number of children. _____

Given name	Date of birth	Country of birth	Date of entry	Port of entry	Location	Alien Registration No.	Sex
							☐ Male ☐ Female
							☐ Male ☐ Female
							☐ Male ☐ Female
							☐ Male ☐ Female
							☐ Male ☐ Female
							☐ Male ☐ Female
							☐ Male ☐ Female

26. Complete the following with regard to each absence you have had from the United States *for a period of six months or less* since you entered for permanent residence. (If none, write "None".)

Ship, airline, railroad or bus company, or other means used to return to the United States.	Returned at (Place or port of entry)	Date departed	Date returned

27. Complete the following with regard to each absence you have had from the United States *for a period of six months or more* since you entered for permanent residence. (If none, write "None")

Ship, airline, railroad or bus company, or other means used to return to the United States.	Returned at (Place or port of entry)	Date departed	Date returned

28. The law provides that you may not be regarded as qualified for naturalization, if you knowingly committed certain offenses or crimes, even though you may not have been arrested. Have you ever, in or outside the United States:

(If you answer "Yes" to a) or b), give the following information as to each incident.)

a) knowingly committed any crime for which you have not been arrested?

☐ Yes   ☐ No

b) been arrested, cited, charged, indicted, convicted, fined or imprisoned for breaking or violating any law or ordinance, including traffic regulations?

☐ Yes   ☐ No

Where (City, State and Country)	Date of Offense	Nature of Offense	Outcome of case, if any

29. List your present and past membership in or affiliation with every organization, association, fund, foundation, party, club, society or similar group in the United States or in any other place, and your foreign military service (If none, write "None".)

Name of organization	Location of organization	Membership from	Membership to

30. Are you now, or have you ever, in the United States or in any other place, been a member of, or in any other way connected or associated with the Communist Party? (If "Yes", attach full explanation)

☐ Yes   ☐ No

31. Have you ever knowingly aided or supported the Communist Party directly, or indirectly through another organization, group or person? (If "Yes", attach full explanation)

☐ Yes   ☐ No

32. Do you now or have you ever advocated, taught, believed in or knowingly supported or furthered the interests of Communism? (If "Yes", attach full explanation)

☐ Yes   ☐ No

33. During the period March 23, 1933 to May 8, 1945, did you serve in, or were you in any way affiliated with, either directly or indirectly, any military unit, paramilitary unit, police unit, self-defense unit, vigilante unit, citizen unit, unit of the Nazi Party or SS, government agency or office, extermination camp, concentration camp, prisoner of war camp, prison, labor camp, detention camp or transit camp, under the control or affiliated with:

a) the Nazi Government of Germany?

☐ Yes   ☐ No

b) any Government in any area occupied by, allied with, or established with the assistance or cooperation of, the Nazi Government of Germany?

☐ Yes   ☐ No

34. During the period of March 23, 1933 to May 8, 1945, did you ever order, incite, assist, or otherwise participate in the persecution of any person because of race, religion, national origin, or political opinion?

☐ Yes   ☐ No

35. Were you born with, or have you acquired in some way, any title or order of nobility in any foreign state?

☐ Yes   ☐ No

36. Have you ever been declared legally incompetent or have you ever been confined as a patient in a mental institution?

☐ Yes   ☐ No

37. Are deportation proceedings pending against you, or have you ever been deported or ordered deported, or have you ever applied for suspension of deportation?

☐ Yes   ☐ No

38. When was your last federal income tax return filed?

(year) _____

39. Since becoming a permanent resident of the United States, have you filed an income tax return as a nonresident? (If "Yes", explain fully).

☐ Yes   ☐ No

40. Since becoming a permanent resident of the United States, have you failed to file an income tax return because you regarded yourself as a nonresident? (If "Yes", explain fully).

☐ Yes   ☐ No

41. Have you ever claimed in writing, or in any other way, to be a United States citizen?
☐ Yes ☐ No

42. Have you ever deserted from the military, air or naval forces of the United States?
☐ Yes ☐ No

43. Have you ever left the United States to avoid being drafted into the Armed Forces of the United States?
☐ Yes ☐ No

44. Do you believe in the Constitution and form of government of the United States?
☐ Yes ☐ No

45. Are you willing to take the full oath of allegiance to the United States? (See instruction #5)
☐ Yes ☐ No

46. If the law requires it, are you willing to bear arms on behalf of the United States? (If "No", attach a full explanation)
☐ Yes ☐ No

47. If the law requires it, are you willing to perform noncombatant services in the Armed Forces of the United States? (If "No", attach a full explanation)
☐ Yes ☐ No

48. If the law requires it, are you willing to perform work of national importance under civilian direction? (If "No", attach a full explanation)
☐ Yes ☐ No

49. Did you ever apply for exemption from military service because of alienage, conscientious objections, or other reasons? (If "Yes", attach a full explanation)
☐ Yes ☐ No

50. Did you ever register under United States Selective Service laws or draft laws? (If "Yes", complete the following)
☐ Yes ☐ No

Date registered	
Selective Service Number	
Local Board Number	
Present classification	

51. The law provides that you may not be regarded as qualified for naturalization, if, at *any* time during the period for which you are required to prove good moral character, you have been a habitual drunkard; advocated or practiced polygamy; have been a prostitute or procured anyone for prostitution; have knowingly and for gain helped any alien to enter the United States illegally; have been an illicit trafficker in narcotic drugs or marijuana; have received your income mostly from illegal gambling, or have given false testimony for the purpose of obtaining any benefits under this Act. Have you ever, *anywhere*, been such a person or committed any of these acts? (If you answer yes to any of these, attach full explanation.)
☐ Yes ☐ No

You may, by law, change your name at the time you are naturalized. If you wish to do so, please print or type that name below, or the name you want your certificate of naturalization issued under.

This block is to be completed by the person preparing form, if other than the applicant.

I declare that this document was prepared by me at the request of the applicant and is based on all information of which I have any knowledge.

Signature

X

Address

Telephone Number   Date

Signature of Applicant

X

Mailing Address

Telephone Number   Date

Do not fill in blanks below these lines: This application must be sworn to before an offficer of the Immigration and Naturalization Service.

AFFIDAVIT

I do swear that I know the contents of this application, comprising pages 1 to 4, inclusive, and the supplemental forms thereto,

(Form Numbers _____)
subscribed to by me; that the same are true to the best of my knowledge and belief; that corrections numbered:

_____ to _____

were made by me or at my request, and that this application was signed by me with my full, true and correct name, so help me God.

_____
(Complete and true signature of applicant)
(Demonstrate applicant's ability to write English)

Non Filed

(Date, reasons)

Subscribed and sworn to before me by applicant at the preliminary investigation

_____

At _____

This _____ day of _____, 19 _____

I certify that before verification of the above applicant stated in my presence he or she had (heard) read the foregoing application, corrections therein and supplemental form(s) and understood the contents thereof.

_____
(Naturalization Examiner)

THESE FORMS ARE OBSOLETE. YOU CAN GET THE CORRECT FORMS AT YOUR NEAREST NATURALIZATION OFFICE

U.S. GOVERNMENT PRINTING OFFICE: 1986-168-414

U.S. Department of Justice

Immigration and Naturalization Service

BIOGRAPHIC INFORMATION

OMB No. 1115-0066

(Family name)	(First name)	(Middle name)	☐ MALE ☐ FEMALE	BIRTHDATE(Mo.-Day-Yr.)	NATIONALITY	FILE NUMBER A

ALL OTHER NAMES USED (Including names by previous marriages)	CITY AND COUNTRY OF BIRTH	SOCIAL SECURITY NO. (If any)

	FAMILY NAME	FIRST NAME	DATE, CITY AND COUNTRY OF BIRTH(If known)	CITY AND COUNTRY OF RESIDENCE.
FATHER				
MOTHER(Maiden name)				

HUSBAND(If none, so state) OR WIFE	FAMILY NAME (For wife, give maiden name)	FIRST NAME	BIRTHDATE	CITY & COUNTRY OF BIRTH	DATE OF MARRIAGE	PLACE OF MARRIAGE

FORMER HUSBANDS OR WIVES(if none, so state)

FAMILY NAME (For wife, give maiden name)	FIRST NAME	BIRTHDATE	DATE & PLACE OF MARRIAGE	DATE AND PLACE OF TERMINATION OF MARRIAGE

APPLICANT'S RESIDENCE LAST FIVE YEARS. LIST PRESENT ADDRESS FIRST.

STREET AND NUMBER	CITY	PROVINCE OR STATE	COUNTRY	FROM MONTH	YEAR	TO MONTH	YEAR
						PRESENT TIME	

APPLICANT'S LAST ADDRESS OUTSIDE THE UNITED STATES OF MORE THAN ONE YEAR

STREET AND NUMBER	CITY	PROVINCE OR STATE	COUNTRY	FROM MONTH	YEAR	TO MONTH	YEAR

APPLICANT'S EMPLOYMENT LAST FIVE YEARS. (IF NONE, SO STATE) LIST PRESENT EMPLOYMENT FIRST

FULL NAME AND ADDRESS OF EMPLOYER	OCCUPATION(SPECIFY)	FROM MONTH	YEAR	TO MONTH	YEAR
				PRESENT TIME	

Show below last occupation abroad if not shown above. (Include all information requested above.)

THIS FORM IS SUBMITTED IN CONNECTION WITH APPLICATION FOR. ☐ NATURALIZATION ☐ OTHER (SPECIFY): ☐ STATUS AS PERMANENT RESIDENT	SIGNATURE OF APPLICANT	DATE

Are all copies legible? ☐ Yes

IF YOUR NATIVE ALPHABET IS IN OTHER THAN ROMAN LETTERS, WRITE YOUR NAME IN YOUR NATIVE ALPHABET IN THIS SPACE:

PENALTIES: SEVERE PENALTIES ARE PROVIDED BY LAW FOR KNOWINGLY AND WILLFULLY FALSIFYING OR CONCEALING A MATERIAL FACT.

APPLICANT: BE SURE TO PUT YOUR NAME AND ALIEN REGISTRATION NUMBER IN THE BOX OUTLINED BY HEAVY BORDER BELOW.

COMPLETE THIS BOX (Family name)	(Given name)	(Middle name)	(Alien registration number)

Form G-325 (Rev. 10-1-82) Y

EARLY U.S. HISTORY

Christopher Columbus

Reading

Christopher Columbus was born in Italy. He sailed for the king and queen of Spain. He was looking for a new way to India. In 1492 Columbus discovered America. He named the people he found there "Indians" because he thought he was in India. Many Spaniards followed Columbus to Central and South America. They wanted to find gold and to teach the Indians about their church.

Practice words and questions

A. Can you say and understand these words? Find and underline them in the reading.

America	find / found	Indians	Spain / Spaniards
church	gold	Italy	
discover/ed	India	people	

B. Choose a word from the list above to complete each sentence.
1. Columbus ———— America.
2. People from ————came after him.
3. The Spaniards wanted ———— .
4. They wanted to teach the Indians about their ———— .

C. Think about these questions. Can you answer them?
1. In what country was Columbus born?
2. Which king and queen did he sail for?
3. What was Columbus looking for?
4. What did he discover?
5. Why did many Spaniards go to America after Columbus?

The First English Settlements

Reading

The English people came to America with their families looking for freedom. The first English settlements in America were at Jamestown, Virginia (in 1607) and Plymouth, Massachusetts (in 1620). Virginia and Massachusetts were colonies of England.

The people who began Jamestown wanted freedom to work and to make a good life for themselves and their families.

The people who began Plymouth were called Pilgrims. They wanted freedom of religion (their own church). They came in the winter on a ship called the *Mayflower*. The Indians helped them find food and build houses.

Practice words and questions

A. Can you say and understand these words? Find and underline them in the reading.

church	Jamestown, Virginia	religion
colony/ies	*Mayflower*	settlement/s
England/English	Pilgrims	
freedom	Plymouth, Massachusetts	

B. Choose a word from the list above to complete each sentence.
1. _____ , _____ and _____ , _____ were the first English settlements.
2. A _____ is the beginning of a small town.
3. The English people came to America looking for _____ .
4. The _____ came to America looking for freedom of religion.
5. The Pilgrims came to America on a ship called the _____ .
6. Virginia and Massachusetts were _____ of England.

C. Think about these questions. Can you answer them?
1. Did the English people bring their families to America?
2. Why did the first English people come to Jamestown?
3. What time of year was it when the Pilgrims landed?
   How did they stay alive?
4. What is a colony?
   How is it different from a state?

Thanksgiving

Reading

Each year on the fourth Thursday in November, Americans celebrate Thanksgiving Day. It is a day when people give thanks for the good things in life. Many American families eat a special dinner on this day.

The idea of having this holiday came from the Pilgrims. They came from England to America in 1620 to find freedom of religion. Life was very difficult because they arrived in winter. The Indians gave them food and showed them how to build Indian houses.

After one year in America the Pilgrims planned a big dinner. They invited the Indians who had helped them. They celebrated America's first Thanksgiving Day in 1621 by eating the native foods the Indians had shown them: turkey, corn, pumpkin, cranberries, and nuts.

Practice words and questions

A. Can you say and understand these words? Find and underline them in the reading.

celebrate/d	difficult	Indians	nuts	special
corn	dinner	invited	Pilgrims	turkey
cranberries	holiday	native	pumpkin	

B. Choose a word from the list above to complete each sentence.
   1. The fourth Thursday in November is a _____ called Thanksgiving.
   2. Thanksgiving is a _____ day when we give thanks for the good things we have in life.
   3. The _____ celebrated the first Thanksgiving.
   4. The Pilgrims invited the _____ to a dinner.
   5. They ate native foods that they had learned about from the Indians: _____ , _____ , _____ , and _____ .

C. Think about these questions. Can you answer them?
   1. Why do Americans celebrate Thanksgiving Day?
   2. Where did the Pilgrims come from?
   3. Why did they come to America?
   4. Why did they need help from the Indians?

The Growth of the Colonies and Trouble with England

Reading

By 1733 there were 13 English colonies. From north to south they were: New Hampshire, Massachusetts, Connecticut, Rhode Island, Pennsylvania, New Jersey, New York, Delaware, Maryland, Virginia, North Carolina, South Carolina, and Georgia.*

For almost 100 years the kings of England had allowed people from England and many other countries in Europe to come and live in the 13 English colonies. In America life was difficult, but it became easier as the people learned to live and work together. Then in the 1730s, the king of England began to make the American colonists pay very high taxes. The Americans became very unhappy. They sent letters and people to England to explain why the taxes were too high. But the king would not listen.

Some Americans in Boston, Massachusetts wanted to protest the high taxes. They dressed up like Indians, climbed onto an English ship carrying tea, and threw all the tea into Boston harbor. This protest was called the Boston Tea Party.

---

* See the shaded area on the map on pp. 6-7

Practice words and questions

A. Can you say and understand these words? Find and underline them in the reading.

Americans	country/ies	harbor	taxes
Boston Tea Party	England/ English	protest	tea
colonists	Europe	ship	throw/threw

B. Choose a word from the list above to complete each sentence.
   1. The people in the 13 English colonies came from many countries in _____ .
   2. The king of _____ wanted the colonists to pay high taxes.
   3. Some Americans threw English _____ into Boston harbor.
   4. They wanted to _____ the high taxes.
   5. This was called the _____ .

C. Think about these questions. Can you answer them?
   1. What were the first 13 colonies? Find them, from north to south, on the map on pp. 6-7.
   2. What made life easier for the people in the English colonies?
   3. Why did life get more difficult after 1730?
   4. Why did the Americans in the Boston Tea Party dress up like Indians?
   5. What was the Boston Tea Party?

The Revolutionary War

Reading

The English soldiers in America could not find and arrest the people in the Boston Tea Party. The king of England was angry. He closed Boston harbor so that all the people in Boston would pay for the tea. Americans in <u>all</u> the colonies were afraid he would close their harbors too. Leaders of the colonies went to a meeting in Philadelphia. They all voted to stop trade with England.

This made the king even more angry. He sent more soldiers to make the Americans obey his laws. Fighting between English soldiers and American colonists began in Massachusetts.

Many people in the 13 colonies wanted to break away from England. Their leaders voted to fight against England. They wanted a new, independent country. This was the beginning of the Revolutionary War (War of Independence). George Washington was named the commander-in-chief of the Americans. He began to build an army. After six long years of fighting, the Americans won the war and their independence. The colonies became the 13 original states.

Practice words and questions

A. Can you say and understand these words? Find and underline them in the reading.

angry	independent	Revolutionary War
arrest	leaders	soldiers
country	meeting	trade
George Washington	original	voted
harbor	Philadelphia	win/won

B. Choose a word from the list above to complete each sentence.
1. After the Boston Tea Party the king of England was _____ .
2. He wanted his soldiers to _____ the people in the Boston Tea Party.
3. The king closed Boston _____ .
4. _____ from the 13 colonies had a meeting in Philadelphia.
5. Some Americans wanted a new _____ .
6. The first war between England and America was called the _____ .
7. _____ was named commander-in-chief of the Americans.
8. The Americans _____ the war.

C. Think about these questions. Can you answer them?
1. What does "independent" mean?
2. Why were the Americans in <u>all</u> the colonies afraid of the king?
3. How many original states were there?
4. What is another name for the Revolutionary War?

The Declaration of Independence

Reading

After the beginning of the Revolutionary War one leader, Thomas Jefferson, wrote the Declaration of Independence. It explained why the Americans were fighting against England.

It also said the Americans wanted their own country. They believed that "all men are created equal." They wanted the government to protect their rights to "life, liberty and the pursuit of happiness" under the law.

In Philadelphia, leaders of all the colonies signed the Declaration of Independence on July 4, 1776. This date is now called Independence Day. It is the birthday of the United States. The Americans fought the Revolutionary War to get their freedom and the kind of government they wanted.

Practice words and questions

A. Can you say and understand these words? Find and underline them in the reading.

birthday	July 4, 1776	rights
Declaration of Independence	liberty	sign/ed
equal	Philadelphia	Thomas Jefferson
fight/fought	protect	

B. Choose a word from the list above to complete each sentence.
   1. _____ wrote the Declaration of Independence.
   2. The _____ explained why the Americans wanted their own country.
   ➡ 3. The Americans signed the Declaration of Independence on _____ .
   ➡ 4. July 4, 1776 was the _____ of the United States.
   5. The Americans wanted all men to be_____ under their government.
   6. They wanted the government to protect their _____ .
   7. The Americans _____ a war to get their freedom.

C. Think about these questions. Can you answer them?
   ➡ 1. When was the Declaration of Independence signed?
   ➡ 2. Why is that date important?
   3. What kind of government did the Americans want?

The First U.S. Government (1781-1787)

Reading

The first national government of the United States had a Congress, but it could only make laws. The plan of government in the first constitution, called the Articles of Confederation, had no President to enforce laws, no courts to explain laws, no one to collect taxes, no money, and no power.

The states and the people were afraid of their government. Therefore, the first national government of the United States was very weak. This was a dangerous situation because England and Spain could take the land away from the Americans.

In 1787, George Washington called representatives from the original 13 states to a meeting in Philadelphia. They wanted to improve the government. They wrote a new plan of government—the Constitution of the United States.

Practice words and questions

A. Can you say and understand these words? Find and underline them in the reading.

afraid	enforce	leave	power
Congress	explain	make	President
courts	government	money	representatives
dangerous	improve	national	weak

B. Choose a word from the list above to complete each sentence.
   1. The first U.S. government had no _____ , no _____ , and no _____ .
   2. It was a _____ government.
   3. A _____ could make laws.
   4. The states were afraid to give power to the _____ government.

C. Think about these questions. Can you answer them?
   1. Why was it dangerous to have a weak government?
   2. Why did George Washington plan a meeting in Philadelphia in 1787?
   3. Who came to the meeting?
   4. What did they do at that meeting?

The Writing of the Constitution

Reading

In 1787, representatives of the 13 states wrote a new Constitution in Philadelphia. The Constitution of the United States was adopted in 1788 by a vote of a majority of the states. The new government began in 1789.

The principles of the Constitution were liberty, equality, and justice for all. The Constitution is the highest law and plan of government of the United States.

This written Constitution was the highest law which everyone, including <u>all</u> government officers, had to follow. Power was balanced between the national government and the states. The government had three *parts* or *branches*. Each part was given a special job and special powers to check the other parts. In this way, the Constitution provided checks and balances in government power. The government under the Constitution was a great improvement over the first government.

Under the Constitution, George Washington became the first President of the United States.

Practice words and questions

A. Can you say and understand these words? Find and underline them
   in the reading.

adopted	equality	majority	principles
balance/s	improvement	must/has to/had to	representatives
check/s	justice	Philadelphia	
Constitution	liberty	power	

B. Choose a word from the list above to complete each sentence.
   1. The ———— is the highest law and plan of government in the United
      States.
   2. The Constitution was written in the city of ————.
   3. The Constitution was ———— by a vote of a majority of the 13 states.
   4. The Constitution used checks and balances in government ————.
   5. People vote for ———— to take their place in the government.
   6. The new government was a great ———— over the first government.
   7. The ———— of the Constitution are liberty, equality, and justice.

C. Think about these questions. Can you answer them?
   ➡ 1. How many parts did the new government have?
   ➡ 2. Who was the first President of the United States?
   ➡ 3. What is our highest law today?
   4. Who must follow the laws in the United States?
   ➡ 5. What are the principles of the Constitution?
   6. Among what groups is government power divided in the
      United States?

The U.S. Flag and the Pledge of Allegiance

Reading

Every country has a flag. When the 13 colonies declared their independence, they needed a new flag. There is a story that George Washington designed the flag and asked a friend, Mrs. Betsy Ross, to make it for him.

This flag had three colors: red (for courage), white (for truth), and blue (for justice). There were 13 stars in a circle on a blue field and 13 red and white stripes. The number of stars and stripes stood for the number of states at the beginning of the United States.

Today the United States has the same flag but there are 50 stars for the 50 states. The 13 stripes still stand for the first 13 states.

People show their respect for the flag and for the United States when they say the Pledge of Allegiance to the flag:

> *I pledge allegiance to the flag of the United States of America*
> *and to the republic for which it stands, one nation, under God,*
> *indivisible, with liberty and justice for all.*

The flag stands not only for the country (the United States of America) but also for the people, the land, and the government—a republic. A republic is a government elected by the people.

Practice words and questions

A. Can you say and understand these words and numbers? Find and underline them in the reading.

13	flag	liberty	republic	states
50	indivisible	nation	respect	stripes
allegiance	justice	pledge	stars	three (3)

B. Choose a word or number from the list above to complete each sentence.
   1. Today the flag of the United States has _____ stars and _____ stripes.
   2. The_____ stand for the number of states today.
   3. The_____ stand for the number of states at the beginning of the United States.
   4. The U.S. government is a _____ .
   5. A _____ is a government elected by the people.

C. Think about these questions. Can you answer them?
   1. What are the colors in the U.S. flag?
   2. What does the flag stand for?
   3. Why do we say the Pledge of Allegiance?

George Washington

Reading

George Washington was born in Virginia in 1732. His father was an educated landowner and farmer. George Washington did not go to school because there were no schools nearby. He got a good education from his father and brother. He also learned how to farm the land and how to live in the woods. He fought against the Indians with the English army to protect the colonists. He was elected to the Virginia Congress (House of Burgesses).

George Washington became the commander-in-chief of the Americans in the Revolutionary War. Everyone thought it was impossible for the Americans to win the war. The English had the best army and navy in the world. The Americans had no army or navy at the beginning of the war. Military officers from Germany and France helped teach the Americans how to fight against the English. George Washington also taught the Americans to fight like the Indians. Under him the Americans did the impossible. They won the war.

George Washington returned to his farm at the end of the war in 1783. The first government of the United States had no President. This government was not a good government. In 1787 George Washington called a meeting to make a new, better government. A new Constitution, the highest law and plan of government, was written.

In 1789 the Americans elected George Washington to be the first President of the United States. He served two terms. He died in December, 1799. George Washington is often called "the Father of Our Country" for the many ways he helped in the creation of the United States.

➡ 1. First President: George Washington (1789-1797)
2. Second President: John Adams (1797-1801)
3. Third President: Thomas Jefferson (1801-1805)

Practice words and questions

A. Can you say and understand these words? Find and underline them
in the reading.

born	first	served
commander–in–chief	landowner	teach/taught
Constitution	President	terms
education	Revolutionary War	think/thought
elected		

B. Choose a word from the list above to complete each sentence.
1. George Washington's father was a _____.
2. George Washington was the _____ of the Americans in the
   Revolutionary War.
3. George Washington _____ the Americans to fight like the Indians.
4. George Washington called a meeting at which a new _____ was
   written.
5. In 1789 the people in the United States _____ George Washington
   to be President.
➥ 6. He was the _____ President of the United States.
7. He served two _____ .

C. Think about these questions. Can you answer them?
1. What did George Washington do as a young man that helped him in
   the Revolutionary War?
2. Who helped the Americans in the war?
3. Why did everyone think it was impossible for the Americans to win
   the Revolutionary War?

The National Anthem

Reading

The national anthem (song) is " The Star-Spangled Banner." It was written about the U.S. flag by an American named Francis Scott Key. He was arrested by the English in the second war between the English and the Americans, the War of 1812. Mr. Key was held on an English ship during a night battle. He was not an American soldier, so he was not locked up. He was free to move around the ship and watch the fighting.

The English had already burned Washington, D.C. They were trying to take a nearby American fort. They were shooting at it from their ships in the harbor. Mr. Key watched the battle all night. At each flash of gunfire, he looked to see if the American flag was still flying over the fort. In the morning the U.S. flag was still there. Mr. Key knew that the Americans had won the battle, and he was very happy. He wrote a song about watching the battle from an English ship. The song became the national anthem of the United States. Here are the words:

> *Oh! say, can you see, by the dawn's early light,*
> *What so proudly we hailed at the twilight's last gleaming?*
> *Whose broad stripes and bright stars, through the perilous fight,*
> *O'er the ramparts we watched were so gallantly streaming?*
> *And the rockets' red glare, the bombs bursting in air,*
> *Gave proof through the night that our flag was still there.*
> *Oh! say, does that star-spangled banner yet wave*
> *O'er the land of the free and the home of the brave?*

Practice words and questions

A. Can you say and understand these words? Find and underline them in the reading.

American	banner	flag	ship
anthem	battle	fort	Washington, D.C.
arrested	English	Francis Scott Key	

B. Choose a word from the list above to complete each sentence.
1. The national song is also called the national _____ .
2. _____ wrote "The Star-Spangled Banner."
3. He was an _____ citizen being held on an _____ ship.
4. Mr. Key was _____ by the English in the War of 1812.
5. The English were shooting at an American _____ .
6. Another word for flag is _____ .
7. Mr. Key watched all night to see if the _____ was still flying over the American fort.

C. Think about these questions. Can you answer them?
➡ 1. What is the name of the U.S. national anthem? What does the name mean?
2. What two countries were fighting a war when the song was written?
3. What city did the English burn during this war?
4. At what time of day did the battle take place?
5. Who won the battle? How did the writer know this?
6. How did Mr. Key feel about his country?

Abraham Lincoln and the Civil War

Reading

Abraham Lincoln, called "Abe," was born in Kentucky on February 12, 1809. His father was a farmer. The family was very poor. They lived very far from cities and schools. Abe taught himself to read. His family moved to Indiana and then to Illinois looking for better land.

When he was 21 years old, Abe left home to live by himself. He was a storekeeper, a surveyor, and a mailman. He was friendly, kind, helpful, and very honest. People liked him and elected him to the Illinois state government in 1834. During this time he taught himself to be a lawyer. Later he was elected Representative from Illinois to the U.S. Congress in Washington, D.C.

Abe Lincoln believed that slavery was wrong. He and his ideas became well known in the U.S. during a series of debates about slavery with Illinois Senator Douglas. In 1860 Abraham Lincoln was elected the 16th President of the United States.

Eleven states in the South broke away from the United States to make a new country. They wanted slavery. The North began to fight against the South in the Civil War. Abraham Lincoln was the leader of the North. The North won the war, which ended on April 9, 1865.

One week later, on April 15, 1865, Abraham Lincoln died. A man who loved the South had shot him. Lincoln is remembered as the President who freed the slaves and saved the Union.

➡ Presidents assassinated (killed) in office:
Abraham Lincoln—April 15, 1865
James Garfield—September 19, 1881
William McKinley—September 14, 1901
John F. Kennedy—November 22, 1963

Practice words and questions

A. Can you say and understand these words? Find and underline them in the reading.

Civil War	honest	save	teach/taught
Congress	North	slavery	Union
debates	poor	slaves	win/won
elect	President	South	wrong

B. Choose a word from the list above to complete each sentence.
   1. One reason people liked Abe Lincoln was that he was _____.
   2. His ideas became known in a series of _____ about slavery with Senator Douglas.
   3. Abe Lincoln thought slavery was _____.
➤ 4. Abraham Lincoln was elected 16th _____ of the United States.
➤ 5. The war between the North and the South was called the _____.
   6. The _____ won the war.
   7. Abe Lincoln was the leader of the _____.
   8. He freed the _____.
   9. He also saved the _____.

C. Think about these questions. Can you answer them?
   1. What kind of education did Lincoln have?
   2. Why did he think slavery was wrong?
   3. What kind of person was Abe Lincoln?
➤ 4. Why is Abraham Lincoln remembered today?

U.S. GOVERNMENT

The Constitution: Our Highest Law and Plan of Government

Reading

The Constitution is our highest law and plan of government.

When the United States began, the people wanted a strong government under the control of the people. They wrote a plan for a republic, a government elected by the people. This plan divided the government into three parts to keep the power in the hands of the people. There is a *legislative* part with a Congress to make laws; there is an *executive* part with a President to enforce laws, and there is a *judicial* part with courts to explain laws.*

It is possible to change the Constitution. A change in the Constitution is called an amendment. To change the Constitution, an amendment must pass both houses of Congress by a two-thirds (2/3) majority vote and then be passed by the state legislatures of three-fourths (3/4) of the states. There are other ways to amend the Constitution, but this is the usual way. The President never signs amendments.

*See the U.S. Government chart on p. 60.

Practice words and questions

A. Can you say and understand these words and numbers? Find and underline them in the reading.

amendment	explains	plan
Constitution	judicial	republic
control	legislative	three (3)
elected	makes	three-fourths (3/4)
enforces	people	two-thirds (2/3)
executive		

B. Choose a word or number from the list above to complete each sentence.

➡ 1. The _____ is the highest law.

➡ 2. The U.S. government is a _____ .

   3. The _____ control the government.

➡ 4. The government is divided into _____ parts.

   5. A change in the Constitution is called an _____ .

➡ 6. The _____ part of government makes laws.

➡ 7. The executive part of government _____ laws.

   8. The _____ part of government explains laws.

C. Think about these questions. Can you answer them?

➡ 1. What kind of government does the United States have?

   2. Why are there three parts in the U.S. government?

   3. How can the Constitution be changed?

   4. Does the President sign amendments?

The Bill of Rights

Reading

In 1789, people did not believe that the three parts of government under the Constitution protected them enough. The people wanted a list of their rights included in the Constitution. They thought the list would help guarantee their freedom. The list of rights became the first ten amendments to the Constitution. They passed together in 1791. These first ten amendments are called the Bill of Rights.

The Bill of Rights protects many of our rights (freedoms). <u>Some</u> of these rights are:

In the *First Amendment*:
- freedom of speech
- freedom of the press
- freedom of religion
- freedom to hold meetings
- freedom to complain to the government

In the *Fourth Amendment*:
- freedom to be safe in your home

In the *Sixth* and *Seventh Amendments*:
- the right to a jury trial

In the *Ninth* and *Tenth Amendments*:
- the rights and powers not in the Constitution belong to the people and the states

Today the Constitution has 27 amendments. The Bill of Rights and the other amendments guarantee the rights of every person in the United States, citizen and non-citizen. The people keep their freedom when their rights are protected.

Practice words and questions

A. Can you say and understand these words and numbers? Find and
underline them in the reading.

Bill of Rights	jury	rights
complain	people	speech
enough	press	states
freedom/s	protect	ten (10)
guarantee	religion	trial

B. Choose a word from the list above to complete each sentence.
➡ 1. The first ten amendments are called the _____.
   2. The Bill of Rights protects _____. (two answers)
   3. The people keep their _____ when their rights are protected.
   4. The government cannot stop what the people say because of their
      freedom of _____.
   5. The government cannot stop what the people write because of their
      freedom of the _____.
   6. The people can believe in any god, or no god, because of their freedom
      of _____.
   7. In U.S. courts, citizens, not judges, decide who has broken the law
      because of the right to a _____ trial.
   8. The rights and powers not in the Constitution belong to the _____ and
      the _____.

C. Think about these questions. Can you answer them?
   1. Why did the people want a list of their rights included in the
      Constitution?
➡ 2. What are some of the rights (freedoms) in the Bill of Rights?
   3. Are the rights in the Bill of Rights only for citizens?
➡ 4. How many amendments to the Constitution are there today?

The Amendments to the U.S. Constitution

Reading

The first ten amendments (the Bill of Rights) were passed all together. The other 17 amendments have been passed separately in the years since the Constitution became the highest law in the United States. Here is a short description of these amendments.

Amendment	Description
Eleven (11)	Federal courts cannot hear cases between a state and a person from another state. (1798)
Twelve (12)	The President and Vice-President are elected by the people and by presidential electors (elected indirectly by the people). (1804)
Thirteen (13)	Slavery is outlawed in the United States. (1865)
Fourteen (14)	Citizenship is given to any person of any race or religion born in the United States or naturalized. (1868)
Fifteen (15)	All citizens have the right to vote. (1870)
Sixteen (16)	Congress has the power to pass laws for an income tax. (1913)
Seventeen (17)	Senators are elected directly by the people. (1913)
Eighteen (18)	All alcoholic drinks are outlawed in the United States (National Prohibition). (1920)
Nineteen (19)	Women have the right to vote. (1920)
Twenty (20)	January 3 is the day Congress begins meeting and January 20 is the day the President takes office. (1933)
Twenty-One (21)	Amendment Eighteen is cancelled. Each state has the right to make its own laws about alcoholic drinks. (1933)
Twenty-Two (22)	The President's term of office is limited to two terms (Eight years, or not more than a total of ten years if he or she was Vice-President and took over part of another president's term). (1951)
Twenty-Three (23)	Residents of Washington, D.C. have the right to vote for President and Vice-President. (1961)
Twenty-Four (24)	Voting is free; no one can be charged a tax to vote. (1964)

Twenty-Five (25)	The Vice-President takes the President's place if the President is disabled.
	Between elections, a new Vice-President can be appointed by the President with the consent of Congress. (1967)
Twenty-Six (26)	Eighteen-year-olds have the right to vote. (1971)
Twenty-Seven (27)	A pay raise for Congress begins only after the next congressional election. (1992)

Practice words and questions

A. Here is a list of amendment numbers:

Eleven (11)	Seventeen (17)	Twenty-Two (22)
Twelve (12)	Eighteen (18)	Twenty-Three (23)
Thirteen (13)	Nineteen (19)	Twenty-Four (24)
Fourteen (14)	Twenty (20)	Twenty-Five (25)
Fifteen (15)	Twenty-One (21)	Twenty-Six (26)
Sixteen (16)		

B. Choose a number from the list above to complete each sentence.
1. Amendment _____ gives the vote to women.
2. Eighteen-year-olds can vote because of Amendment _____ .
3. Amendment _____ gives the vote to all citizens.
4. The President's term is limited by Amendment _____ .
5. Congress can collect income tax because of Amendment _____ .
6. Amendment _____ says any person of any race or religion can become a citizen.

C. Think about these questions. Can you answer them?
1. Who can the residents of Washington, D.C. vote for?
2. How were the slaves freed?
3. Which amendment explains how much it costs to vote?
4. How are U.S. Senators elected?
5. What amendment was cancelled? How was it cancelled? Why?
6. How are the President and Vice-President elected?
7. Who takes the President's place if he or she is disabled? Which amendment explains this?
8. How is a new Vice-President chosen between elections? Which amendment explains this?

The Federal Government: A Republic

Reading

The federal or national government of the United States is a *republic*. A republic is a government elected by the people. A republic is a kind of *democracy*. A democracy is any government controlled by the people.

The Constitution of the United States divides the government into three parts and explains what each part can do. The Bill of Rights gives any powers not in the Constitution to the people and the states in the Tenth Amendment. The laws in the Constitution and the Bill of Rights help the people keep control of the government.

All citizens of the United States 18 years old and over can vote. They elect or vote for people to be their representatives and to work for them in the government. A person becomes a representative of the people if he or she wins a majority of their votes. The U.S. government needs <u>all</u> its citizens to vote so that it will continue to be a government of <u>all</u> the people.

Practice words and questions

A. Can you say and understand these words? Find and underline them in the reading.

control	federal	national	republic
democracy	government	people	vote
elect	majority	representatives	

B. Choose a word from the list above to complete each sentence.
1. Democracy is a government controlled by the _____ .
2. Any government controlled by the people is a _____ .
3. The government of the United States is a _____ .
4. The national government is often called the _____ government.
5. People elected to the government are _____ of the people.
6. To become a representative of the people a person must win a _____ of the people's votes.

C. Think about these questions. Can you answer them?
1. How is a government representative of the people chosen?
2. Why should all U.S. citizens vote?
3. How does the Constitution help the people keep control of the government?

Other Governments: Dictatorships

Reading

Not all governments in the world are controlled by the people. Many governments are controlled by one person or one group of people. These governments are called *dictatorships*.

A dictatorship can be one of the following:

- the government of a king (monarchy)
- the government of one religion or of one religious leader (theocracy)
- a government of nationalistic and militaristic leaders (fascism)
- the government of one political party such as the Communist party (communism)

Most citizens of the United States do <u>not</u> believe in and do <u>not</u> want to live in a dictatorship. They do <u>not</u> believe in communism and do <u>not</u> belong to the Communist party. They want to be free to control their government and their lives. In a dictatorship the people are not free.

Practice words and questions

A. Can you say and understand these words? Find and underline them in the reading.

believe	communism	military
belong	dictatorship	political party

B. Choose a word from the list above to complete each sentence.
   1. A government controlled by one person or group is called a _____ .
   2. _____ is a form of government in which one political party controls.
   3. Most U.S. citizens do not believe in _____ . (2 answers)

C. Think about these questions. Can you answer them?
   1. Are all governments in the world controlled by the people?
   2. Why do U.S. citizens <u>not</u> like dictatorships?
   ➡ 3. Are you a Communist?

Washington, D.C.: The Capital of the United States

Reading

The center and meeting place of the government is the capital, Washington, D.C. The letters "D.C." stand for District of Columbia. The District of Columbia is in the eastern part of the United States between the states of Maryland and Virginia.

The U.S. government has three parts: legislative, or law-making, executive, or law-enforcing, and judicial, or law-explaining. These parts are sometimes called *departments* or *branches*. The people in each part work in different places in Washington, D.C.

Congress makes laws in the Capitol building; the President lives and enforces laws in the White House, and the justices on the Supreme Court explain laws in the Supreme Court building. Each department works separately, but the departments also have powers to check up on each other.

Practice words and questions

A. Can you say and understand these words? Find and underline them in the reading.

branches	check up	eastern	Supreme Court
capital	departments	parts	Washington, D.C.
Capitol	district	separate	White House

B. Choose a word from the list above to complete each sentence.

➡ 1. _____ is the capital of the United States.

2. It is in the _____ part of the United States.

➡ 3. There are three _____ in the U.S. government. (3 answers)

4. The President lives and works in the _____ .

5. Congress works in the _____ .

6. The different departments can _____ on each other.

C. Think about these questions. Can you answer them?

1. What do the letters " D.C." in Washington, D.C. stand for?

➡ 2. How many parts of the government are there? What are they called?

➡ 3. What does each part do?

➡ 4. What does Congress do? What does the President do?

➡ 5. Where do the Supreme Court justices work? What do they do?

Legislative Branch

Reading*

The *legislative* department of the government makes the laws. Legislative means law-making.

The group of people that makes U.S. laws is called Congress. Congress has two parts: the Senate and the House of Representatives. All members of Congress are elected by the people.

The Senate has 100 members, two Senators from each state. Each Senator is elected for six years by all the people of a state. (All Senators are not elected at the same time.)

A Senator must be at least 30 years old and have been a U.S. citizen for nine years. The presiding officer of the Senate is the Vice-President. When he or she is absent, the President pro tempore of the Senate takes his or her place. (The President pro tempore is a Senator chosen by all the other Senators.)

The House of Representatives has 435 members. The number of Representatives from each state depends on the population of the state. Each Representative is elected for two years by the people of his or her district.

A Representative must be at least 25 years old and have been a citizen for seven years. The presiding officer of the House is the Speaker (a Representative chosen by all the other Representatives.)

Each house meets separately, but neither house can make laws alone. An idea for a law is called a bill. A bill must pass both houses of Congress by a majority vote and be signed by the President. Most U.S. laws are made in this way.

The President may veto (refuse to sign) the bill and send it back to Congress. Both houses can then vote on it again. It must pass both houses the second time by a two-thirds (2/3) majority vote. If it passes, the bill becomes law without the President's signature.

(continued)

*See the U.S. Government chart on p. 60.

Legislative Branch (continued)

The Powers of Congress

Congress makes laws. <u>Some</u> of its specific law-making powers listed in the Constitution are:

1. to declare war
2. to provide money for the military
3. to provide money for post offices
4. to provide money for U.S. courts
5. to coin money
6. to pass laws to borrow money
7. to pass laws for Washington, D.C.
8. to pass laws for naturalization
9. to pass laws necessary to carry out other powers
10. to admit new states
11. to regulate interstate and foreign commerce

The powers of the House of Representatives <u>alone</u> without the Senate are:

- to begin a law to raise money
- to bring a bill of impeachment
- to vote for a President when necessary

The powers of the Senate <u>alone</u> without the House of Representatives are:

- to vote on the President's appointments of cabinet officers and of federal judges
- to vote on treaties the President signs
- to hold impeachment trials
- to vote for a Vice-President when necessary

Congress may <u>not</u>:

- spend money except by law
- pass laws to take away the right to see a judge after a person is arrested (except in time of war). This right is called *habeas corpus*.
- pass laws to tax exports

Practice words and questions

A. Can you say and understand these words and numbers? Find and underline them on pages 51–52.

Congress	legislative	President	Speaker
court	majority	Senate	state
four (4)	nine (9)	seven (7)	two (2)
House of Representatives	people	six (6)	Vice-President

B. Choose a word or number from the list above to complete each sentence.
1. The _____ department makes the laws.
2. Congress has _____ parts.
3. There are 100 members in the _____ .
4. There are 435 members in the _____ .
5. Members of Congress are elected by the _____ .
6. Senators serve _____ years and Representatives serve _____ years.
7. The _____ presides over the House of Representatives.
8. There are two Senators from each _____ .

C. Think about these questions. Can you answer them?
➡ 1. Who makes the laws for the United States?
➡ 2. What are the parts of Congress called?
➡ 3. How many Representatives come from each state?
  4. Where does Congress meet?
  5. How is a law made?
  6. What is a majority? What is a two-thirds (2/3) majority?
  7. Who is the Representative from your congressional district?
➡ 8. Who are the U.S. Senators from your state?
  9. Who presides over the Senate when the Vice-President is absent?
  10. What are some of the powers of Congress?
  11. What are some of the powers of the Senate alone?
  12. What are some of the powers of the House of Representatives alone?
  13. What are some of the things Congress may <u>not</u> do?

Executive Branch

Reading*

The *executive* department of the government enforces the laws of the United States. The group of people that enforces the laws includes the President, the Vice-President, and the Cabinet.

The chief executive is the President. The President and the Vice-President are elected indirectly by the people for a term of four years. This means that first the people vote for presidential electors in each state and then the electors vote for President. The number of electors from each state is the same as the number of people in Congress from each state.

The Vice-President takes the President's place when necessary. He or she is also the presiding officer of the Senate. The Vice-President helps the President enforce the laws.

If it is necessary for someone to take the President's place and there is <u>no</u> Vice-President, the Speaker of the House of Representatives will become President. After the Speaker the order of presidential succession continues with the President pro tempore of the Senate and then the members of the Cabinet (see the order of presidential succession on p. 61)

The Constitution gives the qualifications for President. The President must be at least 35 years old, a native-born U.S. citizen, and have lived in the United States for 14 years before his or her election. The Twenty-Second Amendment limits the President to two terms (eight years).

The Constitution also lists the powers and duties of the President. The President enforces the laws, signs and vetoes bills, is commander-in-chief of the military, gives a State of the Union address to Congress each year, appoints Cabinet officers and U.S. judges with the consent of the Senate, signs treaties with the consent of the Senate, and grants pardons. At the beginning of his or her term, the President promises to protect and follow the Constitution.

*See the U.S. Government chart on p. 60.

Practice words and questions

A. Can you say and understand these words and numbers? Find and underline them in the reading.

14	enforce	native-born	Twenty-Second
35	executive	people	Amendment
Cabinet	four (4)	qualifications	two (2)
eight (8)	House of	President	Vice-President
electors	Representatives	Senate	

B. Choose a word or number from the list above to complete each sentence.

➡ 1. The _____ department enforces the laws.

2. The U.S. chief executive is the _____ .

3. The _____ helps the President. (2 answers)

➡ 4. The President must be a _____ citizen.

➡ 5. The President's term is _____ years.

6. The President may serve _____ terms.

7. The President is elected indirectly by the _____ .

C. Think about these questions. Can you answer them?

➡ 1. Who is the head of the executive department?

2. Who takes the President's place when necessary?

➡ 3. What are the qualifications for President?

4. What gives the powers and duties to the President?

5. What must the President promise to do at the beginning of his or her term?

6. What are some of the President's powers?

7. Who checks the President's power?

8. How many electors does your state have?

9. Where does the President live?

➡ 10. Who are the President and Vice-President now?

➡ 11. How did they get their jobs?

The Cabinet

Reading*

The Cabinet is a group of people that helps the President enforce the laws. There are 14 members in the Cabinet. Cabinet members (or officers) are appointed by the President with the consent of the Senate. They hold their offices at the President's pleasure, as long as the President wants them to serve.

The following is a list of the Cabinet offices and the duties of each. Cabinet offices sometimes change. Check to be sure which offices exist and how many there are.

Secretary of State	takes care of foreign relations
Secretary of the Treasury	takes care of money
Secretary of Defense	takes care of military matters
Attorney General	top lawyer of the U.S; is head of naturalization
Secretary of the Interior	in charge of natural resources, government lands and parks
Secretary of Agriculture	in charge of farm problems
Secretary of Commerce	in charge of business affairs
Secretary of Labor	in charge of workers' problems
Secretary of Health and Human Services	takes care of federal social services
Secretary of Housing and Urban Development (HUD)	in charge of federal programs for housing and rebuilding cities
Secretary of Transportation	enforces laws about any means of moving people or things
Secretary of Energy	in charge of federal energy (heat, light, and power) programs
Secretary of Education	in charge of federal programs in education at all levels
Secretary of Veterans Affairs	in charge of services and programs for veterans

*See the U.S. Government chart on p. 60 and the U.S. Government Officers chart on p. 61.

Practice words and questions

A. Can you say and understand these words and numbers? Find and underline them in the reading.

14	veteran	naturalization
Agriculture	Education	President
Attorney General	Energy	Senate
Cabinet	HUD	State
Commerce	Interior	Transportation
Defense	Labor	Treasury

B. Choose a word or number from the list above to complete each sentence.

➡ 1. There are _____ members in the Cabinet.

 2. The Secretary of the _____ takes care of U.S. lands and natural resources.

➡ 3. The _____ is head of naturalization.

 4. The person in charge of foreign affairs is the Secretary of _____.

 5 The Secretary of the _____ takes care of U.S. money.

 6. Business affairs are the job of the Secretary of _____.

 7. The Secretary of _____ is in charge of workers' problems.

 8. The _____ is the top lawyer in the United States.

 9. The Department of _____ is in charge of federal programs in education.

 10. Federal power, heat, and light programs are directed by the Secretary of _____.

 11. Cabinet members help the _____ enforce the laws.

 12. The Secretary of _____ takes care of military matters.

 13. The President appoints Cabinet members with the consent of the _____.

C. Think about these questions. Can you answer them?

 1. What is the Cabinet?

➡ 2. Who is the Attorney General?

 3. How long do Cabinet members serve?

 4. Who is the Secretary of State?

Judicial Branch

Reading*

The *judicial* department of the government explains the laws. The people who explain the laws are called judges. They work in the courts. The federal courts include the U.S. Supreme Court, the Circuit Courts of Appeals, and District Courts.

The Supreme Court was established by the Constitution. Congress has established the other courts since the Constitution was written. Congress can make new courts when necessary.

The U.S. Supreme Court is the highest court. There is one U.S. Supreme Court. It meets in Washington, D.C. Nine judges called justices sit on the U.S. Supreme Court. One of these justices is the Chief Justice of the United States.

The Supreme Court decides cases sent "on appeal" (for review) from lower courts. It also decides if a law is constitutional, that is, if it follows the Constitution. The Supreme Court's decisions are final.

There are 12 Courts of Appeals throughout the United States. Each court decides cases sent on appeal from lower trial courts in its district. As in the Supreme Court, all the judges in each of these courts sit and decide cases together.

District Court is the lowest federal court. It is the federal trial court where almost all cases begin. There are 91 District Courts (94 including courts in U.S. Territories) throughout the United States. Many judges serve each District Court, but a judge always sits alone in a trial.

All federal judges are appointed by the President with the consent of the Senate. They serve for life unless they resign or are impeached.

---

*See the U.S. Government chart on p. 60.

Practice words and questions

A. Can you say and understand these words and numbers? Find and
underline them in the reading.

12	Courts of Appeals	nine (9)
appeal	District Court	Senate
Chief Justice	explains	Supreme Court
Congress	federal	trial
Constitution	judge	Washington, D. C.

B. Choose a word or number from the list above to complete each sentence.

➡ 1. There are _____ justices on the U.S. Supreme Court.

2. _____ is the U.S. trial court where most cases begin.

➡ 3. The highest court is the _____ .

➡ 4. The judicial department _____ the laws.

5. U.S. or national courts are called _____ courts.

6. The U.S. Supreme Court meets in _____ .

7. Federal judges are appointed by the President with the
   consent of the _____ .

8. _____ can make new courts if necessary.

9. The top judge in the U.S. is called the _____ .

C. Think about these questions. Can you answer them?

1. What established the U.S. Supreme Court?

2. How long do federal judges serve?

3. How many U.S. Supreme Courts are there?
   How many U.S. Courts of Appeals?
   How many District Courts in the U.S.?

4. How many judges sit in a trial?

➡ 5. Who is the Chief Justice of the U.S. Supreme Court?

6. Who decides if laws are constitutional?

7. Who makes the final decision about a law in the United States?

U.S. Government: The Three Branches

LEGISLATIVE Makes Laws	EXECUTIVE Enforces Laws	JUDICIAL Explains Laws
CONGRESS **SENATE** (100 Senators) • 2 Senators from each state • elected by the people • term: 6 years A Senator must be: • 30 years old • a citizen for 9 years The presiding officer of the Senate is: • the Vice-President, or • the President pro tempore of the Senate (when the Vice-President is absent) **HOUSE OF REPRESENTATIVES** (435 Representatives) • the *number* of Representatives from each state depends on the population of the state • elected by the people • term: 2 years A Representative must be: • 25 years old • a citizen for 7 years The presiding officer of the House is: • the Speaker of the House	**PRESIDENT** and **VICE-PRESIDENT** • elected by the people and the presidential electors • term: 4 years A President or Vice-President must: • be at least 35 years old • be a native-born citizen • live in the U.S. 14 years before election **CABINET** (14 officers) • appointed by the President with the consent of the Senate • term: at the President's pleasure	**ALL FEDERAL COURTS** **SUPREME COURT** (9 justices) **CIRCUIT COURT OF APPEALS** (11 courts) **DISTRICT COURT** (91* trial courts) • federal judges are appointed by the President with consent of the Senate • term: life *95 including territorial District Courts

U. S. Government Officers

To the student: Fill in the chart below with current information for the U.S. and your state. Ask your teacher or a librarian if you need help.

President _____

[1]**Vice-President** _____

Cabinet:

    [4]Secretary of State _____

    [5]Secretary of the Treasury _____

    [6]Secretary of Defense _____

    [7]Attorney General _____

    [8]Secretary of the Interior _____

    [9]Secretary of Agriculture _____

    [10]Secretary of Commerce _____

    [11]Secretary of Labor _____

    [12]Secretary of Health and Human Services _____

    [13]Secretary of Housing and Urban Development _____

    [14]Secretary of Transportation _____

    [15]Secretary of Energy _____

    [16]Secretary of Education _____

    [17]Secretary of Veterans Affairs _____

Two U.S. Senators (from your state) _____

_____

One U.S. Representative from the ____ Congressional District _____

_____

[3]**President pro tempore of the Senate** _____

[2]**Speaker of the House of Representatives** _____

Chief Justice of the U.S. Supreme Court _____

Small numbers 1–17 show the order of presidential succession

Jury Trial Diagram

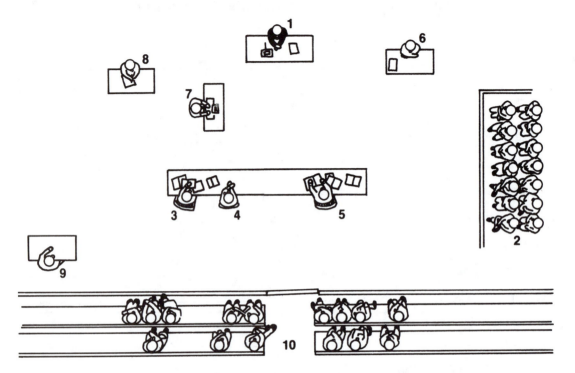

1. **judge**—explains the law and presides over a trial.
2. **jury**—12 citizens (jurors) who listen to the trial and decide if the defendant is *guilty* (<u>did</u> break the law) or *innocent* (did <u>not</u> break the law). At least two alternates sit on the jury in case one of the 12 jurors cannot continue until the end of the trial.
3. **defense**—lawyer who helps the defendant; tries to prove that he or she is innocent.
4. **defendant**—the person on trial, accused of breaking the law.
5. **prosecutor**—lawyer who helps the accusing side; tries to prove that the defendant is guilty.
6. **witness**—has information that is important for the trial.
7. **court reporter**—uses a special shorthand machine to make a record of everything that is said in the trial.
8. **clerk**—serves as secretary of the court room.
9. **guard**—protects the people in the court room.
10. **public**—anybody who wants to watch and listen to the trial.

STATE AND LOCAL GOVERNMENT

State History and Government

Reading*

History and Land of a State

The history and early government of each state are different. The land of each state is also different. A state might have mountains, rivers, or lakes that are important. Some events in a state's history have influenced life as it is lived there today.

In taking the naturalization exam, it is important for you to know the name of your state, the date it entered the Union (became a state), its first European settlers, its largest cities, and its capital city.

Rights of the States

The U.S. Constitution in the Tenth Amendment gives to the states and the people all the powers and rights that are not given to the U.S. government. This means that state governments can make, enforce, and explain laws about many things. They can make laws about family relationships, education, and the use of land. That is why laws about marriage, divorce, schools, and property are different from state to state.

The Constitution also says there are a few things states may not do, such as coin money, tax imports and exports, or fight wars with other states and countries.

A New State

To make a new state, the people of the state have to write a state constitution that is then accepted by a vote of the U.S. Congress. This constitution becomes the state's highest law and plan of government. It must be in agreement with the U.S. Constitution.

Government

All state governments have three parts, and all states except Nebraska have a two-part legislative branch. The executive branch includes a Governor and several other officers. The judicial branch includes the highest court and several lower courts.

The citizens of a state vote for many state government officers. You should know who represents you in the state legislative branch and who your Governor is.

---

* Fill in the chart on p. 70 with information about your state.

Practice words and questions

A. Can you say and understand these words? Find and underline them in the reading.

capital	lakes	plan	states
education	mountains	represents	Union
influenced	naturalization	rivers	

B. Choose a word from the list above to complete each sentence.
   1. The _____ make laws about family life.
   2. There are many _____ and _____ that are important waterways in the United States.
   3. You must pass the _____ exam to become a citizen.
   4. The history of a state has _____ life in the state today.
   5. The United States is a _____ of 50 states.
   6. The states have schools so that all people can get an _____ .
   7. The highest places in the United States are on the tops of _____ .

C. Think about these questions. Can you answer them?
➡ 1. What is the name of your state? Find it on the U.S. map on pp. 6–7.
   2. Name some important mountains, lakes or rivers in your state. Are there other things about the land in your state that are important?
   3. Where did the first Europeans in your state come from?
   4. What were some important events in the state's history?
➡ 5. When did your state enter the Union?
➡ 6. What are some of the big cities in your state? What is the capital city?
   7. How many *counties* (*parishes, boroughs*) does your state have?
   8. Who represents you in your state legislative branch?
   9. Who is your Governor?

_____

(For information about your state, see "The 50 States" in the Appendices, pp. 74–82.)

County Government

Reading*

The federal and state governments are the big governments in the United States. Each state also has many smaller governments. These smaller governments take care of local needs. "Local" means "close to home." Local governments take care of people with needs that the bigger state governments cannot handle.

<u>Organization</u>

All state land, except a few special pieces, is divided into *counties*. Some states call a county a *parish* or *borough*. Most counties have a Charter or a plan of county government and powers. This Charter must be approved by the legislative branch of the state government.

<u>Government</u>

A group of elected county officers usually has legislative and most of the executive powers in the county. The people in the county vote for these officers and for several others, such as Sheriff, Tax Assessor, and Recorder. The Sheriff is the head of the county police, provides guards for the county courts, and takes care of the county jail. The Tax Assessor decides the value of county land, and collects county taxes. The Recorder keeps track of marriages, births, deaths, and voters in the county.

<u>Services</u>

Counties provide many services. County governments enforce state laws in local areas. They distribute federal and state money to the poor and disabled; they contribute to the local school systems; they take care of county roads, parks, and county lands (property).

Most counties provide health services for people who cannot pay for a doctor or for hospital care. Often the state trial court is a county court. Some counties spend money on public libraries, fire protection, police, and county jails.

<u>Money</u>

County governments receive their money mostly from property taxes and from fees for county services. State and federal governments provide money for education programs and the local courts. States pay for much of the state law enforcement done by the counties.

---

* Fill in the chart on p. 70 with information about your county, borough, or parish.

Practice words and questions

A. Can you say and understand these words? Find and underline them in the reading.

approved	disabled	libraries	Sheriff
Charter	distribute	local	services
collects	fees	property	value
contribute	jail	provide	

B. Choose a word from the list above to complete each sentence.
   1. The _____ is the head of the county police.
   2. The plan of county government is called a _____ .
   3. _____ means "close to home."
   4. Counties _____ federal and state money to people who cannot take care of themselves.
   5. The Tax Assessor _____ county taxes.
   6. Counties often charge _____ for their services.
   7. People can borrow books to read at public _____ paid for by the county.
   8. Most county money comes from _____ taxes and fees.

C. Think about these questions. Can you answer them?
   1. Why do states have local governments?
➡ 2. What is the name of your county, parish, or borough?
   3. What is the name for the group of elected officers who make and enforce your county's laws?
➡ 4. Who is your Sheriff?
   5. What do county governments usually do for people? Does your county do these things?

City Government

Reading*

Organization

Another common local government is city government. City government is often called municipal government. "Municipal" means "city." Cities, like counties, have Charters that must be approved by the state government.

Government

Most U.S. cities have a Mayor, a City Manager or Administrator to take care of day-to-day city business, and a City Council. These positions are organized into two different kinds of city government:

1. In some cities, the Mayor is the chief executive and has the power to enforce city laws.

2. In other cities, the Mayor works in the legislative branch of city government, heads the City Council, and has one vote in the City Council. The City Council makes city laws.

In the second kind of city government, a City Manager has most of the executive power and the Mayor may serve only part-time. In both kinds of city government, the Mayor serves as leader of the city and represents the city in meetings with other governments, businesses, and organizations.

Services

Cities serve citizens in several ways. They provide police, fire, and emergency protection. They keep the city clean through garbage collection and sewer maintenance. They take care of city property, streets, and parks. They often provide libraries, low-cost health care, public transportation, help for the schools, and special services for poor, old, sick, and disabled people. They can regulate building and limit land use to help people keep their neighborhoods safe and pleasant to live in. Some cities have municipal courts that are part of the county courts.

Money

Cities receive some money from federal and state governments for helping carry out state and federal programs. They also get money from the county in which they are located, through property taxes and other taxes collected by the county. Many cities charge fees for their services and collect fines from people who break city laws.

---

* Fill in the chart on p. 70 with information about your city.

Practice words and questions

A. Can you say and understand these words? Find and underline them in the reading.

carry out	emergency	Mayor	organizations
common	fines	Manager	regulate
Council	garbage	municipal	sewer
disabled	located	neighborhoods	transportation

B. Choose a word from the list above to complete each sentence.
   1. City governments are often called ——— governments.
   2. The job of ——— is different in the two kinds of city government.
   3. The ———is the chief executive in the first kind of city government.
   4. The City ——— has most of the executive power in the second kind of city government.
   5. The Mayor is the head of the City ——— in the second kind of city government.
   6. In both kinds of city government, the ——— serves as leader of the city.

C. Think about these questions. Can you answer them?
   1. How do cities serve their citizens?
   2. Where do cities get their money?
   3. What kinds of fees or fines does your city charge?
   4. Is your neighborhood safe and pleasant to live in? Why do you feel this way?
➡ 5. Who is your Mayor?
➡ 6. Who is your City Manager?
➡ 7. Who makes laws for your city?

State and Local Government: The Three Branches

To the student: Fill in the chart with information about your state, county, and city governments. Check the Appendices, pp. 74–82 for information about the 50 states.

	LEGISLATIVE Makes Laws	EXECUTIVE Enforces Laws	JUDICIAL Explains Laws
S T A T E	State _____		
C O U N T Y	County _____		
C I T Y	City _____		

State and Local Government Officers

To the student: Fill in the chart below with the names of the government officers for your state, county, and city. See information on the 50 states in the Appendices (pp. 74–82). Ask your teacher or a librarian if you need help.

STATE: _____

Governor: _____

Lieutenant Governor: _____
State Legislators:

1. _____
       (Legislator's name)   (title)

   from the _____ _____ district
       (number)   (name of upper house)

2. _____
       (Legislator's name)   (title)

   from the _____ _____ district
       (number)   (name of lower house)

Chief Justice: _____

COUNTY: _____

Legislative Group: _____

    number of members: _____

Chief Executive: _____

Sheriff: _____

CITY: _____

City Council (legislative group): _____

    number of members: _____

Mayor: _____

    Does the Mayor work in the legislative branch of city government or is he/she the

    chief executive of the city? _____

City Manager: _____

APPENDICES

The 50 States

The following information about the 50 United States (pp. 74–82) will help you as you read about state and local government (pp. 64–69) and as you fill out the charts on pp. 70–71. Since some of the information may change, be sure to check with your teacher or librarian for the most recent facts.

ALABAMA
Capital: Montgomery
Important Cities: Birmingham, Mobile
Joined the Union: Dec. 14, 1819 (#22)
Counties: 67
U.S. Representatives: 7

State Government
Legislative: Legislature (elected): Senate—35 Senators—4 years; House of Representatives—105 Representatives—4 years
Executive (elected): Governor—4 years; Lieutenant Governor—4 years
Judicial: Supreme Court—9 judges—6 years—elected by the people

ALASKA
Capital: Juneau
Important Cities: Anchorage, Fairbanks
Joined the Union: Jan. 3, 1959 (#49)
Counties (Boroughs): 11
U.S. Representatives: 1

State Government
Legislative: Legislature (elected): Senate—20 Senators—4 years; House of Representatives—40 Representatives—2 years
Executive (elected): Governor—4 years; Lieutenant Governor—4 years
Judicial: Supreme Court—5 judges—10 years—appointed by Governor with consent of the people

ARIZONA
Capital: Phoenix
Important Cities: Tucson, Mesa
Joined the Union: Feb. 14, 1912 (#48)
Counties: 15
U.S. Representatives: 6

State Government
Legislative: Legislature (elected): Senate—30 Senators—2 years; House of Representatives—60 Representatives—2 years
Executive (elected): Governor—4 years; no Lieutenant Governor—Secretary of State succeeds the Governor
Judicial: Supreme Court—5 judges—6 years—appointed by Governor; must be approved by the people after serving 2 years

ARKANSAS
Capital: Little Rock
Important Cities: Fort Smith, Pine Bluff
Joined the Union: June 15, 1836 (#25)
Counties: 75
U.S. Representatives: 4

State Government
Legislative: General Assembly (elected): Senate—35 Senators—4 years; House of Representatives—100 Representatives—2 years
Executive (elected): Governor—2 years; Lieutenant Governor—2 years
Judicial: Supreme Court—7 judges—8 years—elected by the people

CALIFORNIA
Capital: Sacramento
Important Cities: Los Angeles, San Francisco, San Diego
Joined the Union: Sept. 9, 1850 (#31)
Counties: 58
U.S. Representatives: 52

State Government
Legislative: Legislature (elected): Senate—40 Senators—4 years; Assembly—80 Assembly Members—2 years
Executive (elected): Governor—4 years; Lieutenant Governor—4 years
Judicial: Supreme Court—7 judges—12 years—appointed by the Governor with consent of the people

COLORADO
Capital: Denver
Important City: Colorado Springs
Joined the Union: Aug. 1, 1876 (#38)
Counties: 58
U.S. Representatives: 6

State Government
Legislative: General Assembly (elected): Senate—35 Senators—4 years; House of Representatives—65 Representatives—2 years
Executive (elected): Governor—4 years; Lieutenant Governor—4 years
Judicial: Supreme Court—7 judges—10 years—appointed by Governor; must be approved by the people after serving 3 years

CONNECTICUT
Capital: Hartford
Important Cities: Bridgeport, New Haven
Joined the Union: Jan. 9, 1788 (#5)
Counties: 8
U.S. Representatives: 6

State Government
Legislative: General Assembly (elected): Senate—
36 Senators—2 years; House of Representatives—
151 Representatives—2 years
Executive (elected): Governor—4 years; Lieutenant
Governor—4 years
Judicial: Supreme Court—6 judges—8 years—nominated
by the Governor and appointed by the General Assembly

DELAWARE
Capital: Dover
Important Cities: Wilmington, Newark
Joined the Union: Dec. 7, 1787 (#1)
Counties: 3
U.S. Representatives: 1

State Government
Legislative: General Assembly (elected): Senate—
21 Senators—4 years; House of Representatives—
41 Representatives—2 years
Executive (elected): Governor—4 years; Lieutenant
Governor—4 years
Judicial: Supreme Court—5 judges—12 years—appointed
by Governor with consent of the people

FLORIDA
Capital: Tallahassee
Important Cities: Jacksonville, Miami, Tampa
Joined the Union: March 3, 1845 (#27)
Counties: 67
U.S. Representatives: 23

State Government
Legislative: Legislature (elected): Senate—40 Senators—
4 years; House of Representatives—
120 Representatives—2 years
Executive (elected): Governor—4 years; Lieutenant
Governor—4 years
Judicial: Supreme Court—7 judges—6 years—appointed
by Governor

GEORGIA
Capital: Atlanta
Important Cities: Columbus, Savannah
Joined the Union: Jan. 2, 1788 (#4)
Counties: 159
U.S. Representatives: 11

State Government
Legislative: General Assembly (elected): Senate—
56 Senators—2 years; House of Representatives—
180 Representatives—2 years
Executive (elected): Governor—4 years; Lieutenant
Governor—4 years
Judicial: Supreme Court—7 judges—6 years—elected
by the people

HAWAII
Capital: Honolulu
Important City: Hilo
Joined the Union: Aug. 21, 1959 (#50)
Counties: 4
U.S. Representatives: 2

State Government
Legislative: Legislature (elected): Senate—25 Senators—
4 years; House of Representatives—
51 Representatives—2 years
Executive (elected): Governor—4 years; Lieutenant
Governor—4 years
Judicial: Supreme Court—7 judges—10 years—
appointed by the Governor with consent of the Senate

IDAHO
Capital: Boise
Important Cities: Pocatello, Idaho Falls
Joined the Union: July 3, 1890 (#43)
Counties: 44 + small part of Yellowstone National Park
U.S. Representatives: 2

State Government
Legislative: Legislature (elected): Senate—42 Senators—
2 years; House of Representatives—
84 Representatives—2 years
Executive (elected): Governor—4 years; Lieutenant
Governor—4 years
Judicial: Supreme Court—5 judges—6 years—elected
by the people

ILLINOIS
Capital: Springfield
Important Cities: Chicago, Rockford, Peoria
Joined the Union: Dec. 3, 1818 (#21)
Counties: 102
U.S. Representatives: 20

State Government
Legislative: General Assembly (elected): Senate—
59 Senators—4 years (some only 2 years); House
of Representatives—118 Representatives—2 years
Executive (elected): Governor—4 years; Lieutenant
Governor—4 years
Judicial: Supreme Court—7 judges—10 years—elected
by the people

INDIANA
Capital: Indianapolis
Important Cities: Fort Wayne, Gary
Joined the Union: Dec. 11, 1816 (#19)
Counties: 92
U.S. Representatives: 10

State Government
Legislative: General Assembly (elected): Senate—
50 Senators—4 years; House of Representatives—
100 Representatives—2 years
Executive (elected): Governor—4 years; Lieutenant
Governor—4 years
Judicial: Supreme Court—5 judges—10 years—appointed
by Governor; must be approved by the people after
serving 2 years

IOWA
Capital: Des Moines
Important Cities: Cedar Rapids, Davenport
Joined the Union: Dec. 28, 1846 (#29)
Counties: 99
U.S. Representatives: 5

State Government
Legislative: General Assembly (elected): Senate—
50 Senators—4 years; House of Representatives—
100 Representatives—2 years
Executive (elected): Governor—4 years; Lieutenant
Governor—4 years
Judicial: Supreme Court—9 judges—10 years—appointed
by the Governor; must be approved by the people after
serving 1 year

KANSAS
Capital: Topeka
Important Cities: Wichita, Kansas City
Joined the Union: June 29, 1861 (#34)
Counties: 105
U.S. Representatives: 4

State Government
Legislative: Legislature (elected): Senate—40 Senators—
4 years; House of Representatives—
125 Representatives—2 years
Executive (elected): Governor—4 years; Lieutenant
Governor—4 years
Judicial: Supreme Court—7 judges—6 years—elected
by the Governor; must be approved by the people
after serving 1 year

KENTUCKY
Capital: Frankfort
Important Cities: Louisville, Lexington
Joined the Union: June 1, 1792 (#15)
Counties: 120
U.S. Representatives: 6

State Government
Legislative: General Assembly (elected): Senate—
38 Senators—4 years; House of Representatives—
106 Representatives—2 years
Executive (elected): Governor—4 years; Lieutenant
Governor—4 years
Judicial: Supreme Court—7 judges—8 years—elected
by the people

LOUISIANA
Capital: Baton Rouge
Important Cities: New Orleans, Shreveport
Joined the Union: April 30, 1812 (#18)
Counties (Parishes): 64
U.S. Representatives: 7

State Government
Legislative: Legislature (elected): Senate—39 Senators—
4 years; House of Representatives—
105 Representatives—4 years
Executive (elected): Governor—4 years; Lieutenant
Governor—4 years
Judicial: Supreme Court—7 judges—10 years—elected
by the people

MAINE
Capital: Augusta
Important Cities: Portland, Lewiston
Joined the Union: March 15, 1820 (#23)
Counties: 16
U.S. Representatives: 2

State Government
Legislative: Legislature (elected): Senate—35 Senators—
2 years; House of Representatives—
151 Representatives—2 years
Executive (elected): Governor—4 years; no Lieutenant
Governor—President of the Senate succeeds the
Governor
Judicial: Supreme Judicial Court—7 judges—7 years—
appointed by the Governor with consent of the Senate

MARYLAND
Capital: Annapolis
Important Cities: Baltimore, Rockville
Joined the Union: April 28, 1788 (#7)
Counties: 23 + 1 independent city
U.S. Representatives: 8

State Government
Legislative: General Assembly (elected): Senate—
47 Senators—4 years; House of Representatives—
141 Delegates—4 years
Executive (elected): Governor—4 years; Lieutenant
Governor—4 years
Judicial: Court of Appeals—7 judges—10 years—
appointed by the Governor with consent of the Senate;
must be approved by the people after serving 1 year

MASSACHUSETTS
Capital: Boston
Important Cities: Worcester, Springfield
Joined the Union: Feb. 6, 1788 (#6)
Counties: 14
U.S. Representatives: 11

State Government
Legislative: General Court (elected): Senate—
40 Senators—2 years; House of Representatives—
160 Representatives—2 years
Executive (elected): Governor—4 years; Lieutenant
Governor—4 years
Judicial: Supreme Judicial Court—7 judges—serve until
age 70—appointed by the Governor

MICHIGAN
Capital: Lansing
Important Cities: Detroit, Grand Rapids
Joined the Union: June 26, 1837 (#26)
Counties: 83
U.S. Representatives: 16

State Government
Legislative: Legislature (elected): Senate—38 Senators—
4 years; House of Representatives—
110 Representatives—2 years
Executive (elected): Governor—4 years; Lieutenant
Governor—4 years
Judicial: Supreme Court—7 judges—8 years—elected
by the people

MINNESOTA
Capital: St. Paul
Important Cities: Minneapolis, Duluth
Joined the Union: May 11, 1858 (#32)
Counties: 87
U.S. Representatives: 8

State Government
Legislative: Legislature (elected): Senate—67 Senators—
4 years; House of Representatives—
134 Representatives—2 years
Executive (elected): Governor—4 years; Lieutenant
Governor—4 years
Judicial: Supreme Court—9 judges—6 years—elected
by the people

MISSISSIPPI
Capital: Jackson
Important Cities: Biloxi, Hattiesburg
Joined the Union: Dec. 10, 1817 (#20)
Counties: 82
U.S. Representatives: 5

State Government
Legislative: Legislature (elected): Senate—52 Senators—
4 years; House of Representatives—
122 Representatives—4 years
Executive (elected): Governor—4 years; Lieutenant
Governor—4 years
Judicial: Supreme Court—9 judges—8 years—elected
by the people

MISSOURI

Capital: Jefferson City
Important Cities: St. Louis, Kansas City
Joined the Union: Aug. 10, 1821 (#24)
Counties: 115 + 1 independent city
U.S. Representatives: 9

State Government

Legislative: General Assembly (elected): Senate—
34 Senators—4 years; House of Representatives—
163 Representatives—2 years
Executive (elected): Governor—4 years; Lieutenant
Governor—4 years
Judicial: Supreme Court—7 judges—12 years—
appointed by the Governor; must be approved by the
people after serving 1 year

MONTANA

Capital: Helena
Important Cities: Billings, Great Falls
Joined the Union: Nov. 8, 1889 (#41)
Counties: 56 + small part of Yellowstone National Park
U.S. Representatives: 1

State Government

Legislative: Legislature (elected): Senate—50 Senators—
4 years (some 2 years after reapportionment); House of
Representatives—100 Representatives—2 years
Executive (elected): Governor—4 years; Lieutenant
Governor—4 years
Judicial: Supreme Court—7 judges—8 years—elected
by the people

NEBRASKA

Capital: Lincoln
Important Cities: Omaha, Grand Island
Joined the Union: March 1, 1867 (#37)
Counties: 93
U.S. Representatives: 3

State Government

Legislative: Legislature (elected): Legislature—
49 Senators—4 years; no lower house
Executive (elected): Governor—4 years; Lieutenant
Governor—4 years
Judicial: Supreme Court—7 judges—6 years—appointed
by Governor; must be approved by the people after
serving 3 years

NEVADA

Capital: Carson City
Important Cities: Las Vegas, Reno
Joined the Union: Oct. 31, 1864 (#36)
Counties: 17 + 1 independent city
U.S. Representatives: 2

State Government

Legislative: Legislature (elected): Senate—21 Senators—
4 years; Assembly—42 Assembly Members—2 years
Executive (elected): Governor—4 years; Lieutenant
Governor—4 years
Judicial: Supreme Court—5 judges—6 years—elected
by the people

NEW HAMPSHIRE

Capital: Concord
Important Cities: Manchester, Nashua
Joined the Union: June 21, 1788 (#9)
Counties: 10
U.S. Representatives: 2

State Government

Legislative: General Court (elected): Senate—
50 Senators—2 years; House of Representatives—
400 Representatives—2 years
Executive (elected): Governor—4 years; no Lieutenant
Governor—President of the Senate succeeds the
Governor
Judicial: Supreme Court—5 judges—serve until age 70—
appointed by the Governor

NEW JERSEY

Capital: Trenton
Important Cities: Newark, Jersey City
Joined the Union: Dec. 18, 1787 (#3)
Counties: 21
U.S. Representatives: 13

State Government

Legislative: Legislature (elected): Senate—40 Senators—
4 years (some 2 years after reapportionment):
Assembly—80 Assembly Members—2 years
Executive (elected): Governor—4 years: no Lieutenant
Governor—President of the Senate succeeds the
Governor
Judicial: Supreme Court—7 judges—7 years—appointed
by the Governor with consent of the Senate; after
serving 7 years may be reappointed to serve until
age 70

NEW MEXICO
Capital: Santa Fe
Important Cities: Albuquerque, Las Cruces
Joined the Union: Jan. 6, 1912 (#47)
Counties: 33
U.S. Representatives: 3

State Government
Legislative: Legislature (elected): Senate—42 Senators—
4 years; House of Representatives—
70 Representatives—2 years
Executive (elected): Governor—4 years; Lieutenant
Governor—4 years
Judicial: Supreme Court—5 judges—8 years—elected
by the people

NORTH DAKOTA
Capital: Bismark
Important Cities: Fargo, Grand Forks
Joined the Union: Nov. 2, 1889 (#39)
Counties: 53
U.S. Representatives: 1

State Government
Legislative: Legislative Assembly (elected): Senate—
53 Senators—4 years; House of Representatives—
106 Representatives—2 years
Executive (elected): Governor—4 years; Lieutenant
Governor—4 years
Judicial: Supreme Court—5 judges—10 years—elected
by the people

NEW YORK
Capital: Albany
Important Cities: New York City, Buffalo
Joined the Union: July 26, 1788 (#11)
Counties: 62
U.S. Representatives: 31

State Government
Legislative: Legislature (elected): Senate—61 Senators—
2 years: Assembly—50 Assembly Members—2 years
Executive (elected): Governor—4 years; Lieutenant
Governor—4 years
Judicial: Court of Appeals—7 judges—14 years—
appointed by the Governor with consent of the Senate;
after serving 14 years may be reappointed to serve until
age 70

OHIO
Capital: Columbus
Important Cities: Cleveland, Cincinnati
Joined the Union: March 1, 1803 (#17)
Counties: 88
U.S. Representatives: 19

State Government
Legislative: General Assembly (elected): Senate—
33 Senators—4 years; House of Representatives—
99 Representatives—2 years
Executive (elected): Governor—4 years; Lieutenant
Governor—4 years
Judicial: Supreme Court—7 judges—6 years—elected
by the people

NORTH CAROLINA
Capital: Raleigh
Important Cities: Charlotte, Greensboro
Joined the Union: Nov. 21, 1789 (#12)
Counties: 100
U.S. Representatives: 12

State Government
Legislative: General Assembly (elected): Senate—
50 Senators—2 years; House of Representatives—
120 Representatives—2 years
Executive (elected): Governor—4 years; Lieutenant
Governor—4 years
Judicial: Supreme Court—7 judges—8 years—elected
by the people

OKLAHOMA
Capital: Oklahoma City
Important Cities: Tulsa, Lawton
Joined the Union: Nov. 16, 1907 (#46)
Counties: 77
U.S. Representatives: 6

State Government
Legislative: Legislature (elected): Senate—48 Senators—
4 years: House of Representatives—
101 Representatives—2 years
Executive (elected): Governor—4 years: Lieutenant
Governor—4 years
Judicial: Supreme Court—9 judges—6 years: Court
of Criminal Appeals—3 judges—6 years: Judges in
both courts are appointed by the Governor and must
be approved by the people after serving 1 year

OREGON
Capital: Salem
Important Cities: Portland, Eugene
Joined the Union: Feb. 14, 1859 (#33)
Counties: 36
U.S. Representatives: 5

State Government
Legislative: Legislative Assembly (elected): Senate—
30 Senators—4 years; House of Representatives—
60 Representatives—2 years
Executive (elected): Governor—4 years; no Lieutenant
Governor—Secretary of State succeeds the Governor
Judicial: Supreme Court—7 judges—6 years—elected
by the people

PENNSYLVANIA
Capital: Harrisburg
Important Cities: Philadelphia, Pittsburgh
Joined the Union: Dec. 12, 1787 (#2)
Counties: 67
U.S. Representatives: 21

State Government
Legislative: General Assembly (elected): Senate—
50 Senators—4 years; House of Representatives—
203 Representatives—2 years
Executive (elected): Governor—4 years; Lieutenant
Governor—4 years
Judicial: Supreme Court—7 judges—10 years—elected
by the people

RHODE ISLAND
Capital: Providence
Important Cities: Warwick, Cranston
Joined the Union: May 29, 1790 (#13)
Counties: 5
U.S. Representatives: 2

State Government
Legislative: General Assembly (elected): Senate—
50 Senators—2 years; House of Representatives—
100 Representatives—2 years
Executive (elected): Governor—2 years; Lieutenant
Governor—2 years
Judicial: Supreme Court—5 judges—for life—elected
by the General Assembly

SOUTH CAROLINA
Capital: Columbia
Important Cities: Charleston, Greenville
Joined the Union: May 23, 1788 (#8)
Counties: 46
U.S. Representatives: 6

State Government
Legislative: General Assembly (elected): Senate—
46 Senators—4 years; House of Representatives—
124 Representatives—2 years
Executive (elected): Governor—4 years; Lieutenant
Governor—4 years
Judicial: Supreme Court—5 judges—10 years—elected
by the General Assembly

SOUTH DAKOTA
Capital: Pierre
Important Cities: Sioux Falls, Rapid City
Joined the Union: Nov. 2, 1889 (#40)
Counties: 67 (64 county governments)
U.S. Representatives: 1

State Government
Legislative: Legislature (elected): Senate—35 Senators—
2 years; House of Representatives—
30 Representatives—2 years
Executive (elected): Governor—4 years; Lieutenant
Governor—4 years
Judicial: Supreme Court—5 judges—8 years—appointed
by the Governor; must be approved by the people after
serving 3 years

TENNESSEE
Capital: Nashville
Important Cities: Memphis, Knoxville
Joined the Union: June 1, 1796 (#16)
Counties: 95
U.S. Representatives: 9

State Government
Legislative: General Assembly (elected): Senate—
33 Senators—4 years; House of Representatives—
99 Representatives—2 years
Executive (elected): Governor—4 years: President of
the Senate also has the title of Lieutenant Governor—
4 years
Judicial: Supreme Court—5 judges—8 years—elected
by the people

TEXAS
Capital: Austin
Important Cities: Houston, Dallas, San Antonio
Joined the Union: Dec. 29, 1845 (#28)
Counties: 254
U.S. Representatives: 30

State Government
Legislative: Legislature (elected): Senate—31 Senators—
4 years; House of Representatives—
150 Representatives—2 years
Executive (elected): Governor—4 years; Lieutenant
Governor—4 years
Judicial: Supreme Court—9 judges—6 years: Court of
Criminal Appeals—9 judges—6 years: judges in both
courts elected by the people

UTAH
Capital: Salt Lake City
Important Cities: Provo, Ogden
Joined the Union: Jan. 4, 1896 (#45)
Counties: 29
U.S. Representatives: 3

State Government
Legislative: Legislature (elected): Senate—29 Senators—
4 years; House of Representatives—
75 Representatives—2 years
Executive (elected): Governor—4 years; Lieutenant
Governor—4 years
Judicial: Supreme Court—5 judges—10 years—
appointed by the Governor; must be approved
by the people after serving 3 years

VERMONT
Capital: Montpelier
Important Cities: Burlington, Rutland
Joined the Union: March 4, 1791 (#14)
Counties: 14
U.S. Representatives: 1

State Government
Legislative: General Assembly (elected): Senate—
30 Senators—2 years; House of Representatives—
150 Representatives—2 years
Executive (elected): Governor—2 years; Lieutenant
Governor—2 years
Judicial: Supreme Court—5 judges—6 years—appointed
by the Governor with consent of the Senate

VIRGINIA
Capital: Richmond
Important Cities: Norfolk, Virginia Beach
Joined the Union: June 26, 1788 (#10)
Counties: 95 + 41 independent cities
U.S. Representatives: 11

State Government
Legislative: General Assembly (elected): Senate—
40 Senators—4 years; House of Delegates—
100 Delegates—2 years
Executive (elected): Governor—4 years; Lieutenant
Governor—4 years
Judicial: Supreme Court—7 judges—12 years—elected
by the General Assembly

WASHINGTON
Capital: Olympia
Important Cities: Seattle, Spokane
Joined the Union: Nov. 11, 1889 (#42)
Counties: 39
U.S. Representatives: 9

State Government
Legislative: Legislature (elected): Senate—49 Senators—
4 years; House of Representatives—
98 Representatives—2 years
Executive (elected): Governor—4 years; Lieutenant
Governor—4 years
Judicial: Supreme Court—9 judges—6 years—elected
by the people

WEST VIRGINIA
Capital: Charleston
Important Cities: Huntington, Wheeling
Joined the Union: June 20, 1863 (#35)
Counties: 55
U.S. Representatives: 3

State Government
Legislative: Legislature (elected): Senate—34 Senators—
4 years; House of Delegates—100 Delegates—2 years
Executive (elected): Governor—4 years: no Lieutenant
Governor—President of the Senate succeeds the
Governor
Judicial: Supreme Court of Appeals—5 judges—
12 years—elected by the people

WISCONSIN
Capital: Madison
Important Cities: Milwaukee, Green Bay
Joined the Union: May 29, 1848 (#30)
Counties: 72
U.S. Representatives: 9

State Government
Legislative: Legislature (elected): Senate—33 Senators—
    4 years; Assembly—99 Representatives—2 years
Executive (elected): Governor—4 years; Lieutenant
    Governor—4 years
Judicial: Supreme Court—7 judges—10 years—elected
    by the people

WYOMING
Capital: Cheyenne
Important Cities: Casper, Laramie
Joined the Union: July 10, 1890 (#44)
Counties: 23 + Yellowstone National Park
U.S. Representatives: 1

State Government
Legislative: Legislature (elected): Senate—30 Senators—
    4 years; House of Representatives—
    64 Representatives—2 years
Executive (elected): Governor—4 years; no Lieutenant
    Governor; Secretary of State succeeds the Governor
Judicial: Supreme Court—5 judges—8 years—appointed
    by the Governor; must be approved by the people
    after serving 1 year

Sources: *Taylor's Encyclopedia of Government Officials, 1987–88*, Vol. XI, by John Clements, Political Research Inc., Dallas, TX 75248, and *The Book of States*, 1986–87 edition, Council of State Governments, Lexington, KY 40578.

California State History and Government

History

The first people to live in California were Indians. The first European people to come to California were the Spanish; they came from Mexico. The land of California, which was called "Alta (Upper) California," belonged first to the Spanish and then to the Mexicans. Only a few Americans from the East moved to California between 1800 and 1848. The land was not part of the United States until 1848.

The following is an outline of early California history:

1769 The Spanish built a *presidio* (fort) and a *mission* (church) where San Diego now stands. They wanted to stop Russian and English interest in California.

1770 Father Serra and a group of Spanish settlers began a Spanish settlement on Monterey Bay. They built a presidio at Monterey and a mission nearby at Carmel. Monterey became the capital of the Spanish and Mexican governments for Alta California.

1776 A group of Spanish soldiers, missionaries, and colonists started a presidio and a mission at San Francisco.

1781 A group of Spanish people from Mexico began "The City of the Angels" or *Los Angeles*.

1821 The Mexicans won their war for independence from Spain in the same way the Americans had won their independence from England. The Spanish had to leave Mexico, and Mexico took over the government of Alta California

1848 1. Mexico and the United States fought a war about the border between Texas and Mexico. Mexico was weak after its war for independence, and the United States won this war. After the war, the United States took over a large piece of land from Mexico, including the territory of present-day California.

2. James Marshall discovered gold on the property of John Sutter, near Sacramento.

1849 The "Gold Rush" began and thousands of people "rushed" (moved very fast) to California from the East and from all over the world to look for gold. San Francisco and Sacramento became big cities in just a few months.

1850 On September 9, 1850, California became the thirty-first (31st) state of the United States.

The Beginning of U.S. Government in California

The United States took over the government of California in 1848. Many Mexican and American groups were trying to control this government, and things were very confused.

The President appointed a Governor of California in 1849. The Governor then called a meeting of all the different groups to write a Constitution for California. The people at this meeting had many different ideas, and there were many difficult questions to settle. They had a very hard time writing a Constitution. The most important questions were:

1. Should California become a state immediately? They finally decided <u>yes</u>. They wrote a Constitution to send to the U.S. Congress for acceptance.
2. Where should the borders of California be? They agreed on the present borders.
3. Should California allow slavery? They decided there would be no slavery in California.

The Congress of the United States voted to accept California as a state on September 9, 1850. The first California Constitution was very bad, and a new one was written in 1879. This Constitution has been changed more than 200 times (!), but a new one has not been written since 1879.

Legislative Branch

The California Constitution is the highest law of the state. It must agree with the U.S. Constitution. It gives the plan of the state government. California's government is a republic divided into three parts: legislative, executive, and judicial. It meets in the state capital at Sacramento.

The legislative department makes the laws for California. The group of people that makes the laws for California is called the Legislature.

The Legislature is divided into two parts: the Senate and the Assembly. The members of both parts are elected by the people by districts. There are 40 state Senators and 80 Members of the Assembly. The Senators serve four years; the Members of the Assembly serve two years.

The presiding officer of the state Senate is the Lieutenant Governor. One of the Senators is chosen to be the President pro tempore of the Senate. He presides over the Senate when the Lieutenant Governor is absent. The presiding officer of the Assembly is the Speaker, chosen by all the members of the Assembly.

The Legislature makes California laws in the same way that Congress makes national laws: a bill must pass both houses of the Legislature by a majority vote and be signed by the Governor.

Special Powers of the People

A citizen must register his or her name and address before he or she can vote. Any citizen who has registered to vote may write or sign a piece of paper called a *petition*. A petition may ask for a new law or a vote of the people on a law already passed by the Legislature. A petition about a new law is called an *initiative*; a petition for a vote on a law already passed is called a *referendum*.

A registered voter may also start a petition to remove an elected government officer from office. This is called a *recall* petition.

At the time of an election the voters of California vote <u>yes</u> or <u>no</u> on any petition that has been signed by enough registered voters. In this way the people can take part directly in making laws and removing elected government officers.

Executive Branch

The executive branch of the California government enforces the laws of California. The Governor is the chief executive of California. The Lieutenant Governor takes the Governor's place when he or she is not in the state, and presides over the state Senate. The Governor and Lieutenant Governor are elected by the people for four years.

The state Secretary of State, the state Treasurer and the state Attorney General are also part of the executive branch. All of these officers are elected by the people for four years. They are <u>not</u> members of the Governor's Cabinet and do <u>not</u> serve under the Governor. They are elected by the people directly, and they work independently.

The Governor enforces the laws, signs and vetoes bills, grants pardons, and is the chief of the state militia. He or she has a Cabinet, but its members are only advisors.

Judicial Branch

The judicial branch of the California government includes all the state courts. The judges of the state courts explain the laws. The highest state court is called the State Supreme Court. There are seven judges on this court; one of them is the Chief Justice. During the year the Supreme Court meets in three places: Sacramento, San Francisco, and Los Angeles.

There are also five state District Courts of Appeals: in Sacramento, San Francisco, Los Angeles, San Diego, and Fresno. The judges of the State Supreme Court and the appeals courts are appointed by the Governor, with the consent of the people, for twelve years. A majority of the Judiciary Appointments Commission (the Chief Justice of the State Supreme Court, the presiding judge of the State Appeals Court, and the state Attorney General) must agree with the Governor's appointments. The judges may be accepted by a vote of the people for another twelve years.

The state trial court, the lowest state court, is called Superior Court. There is one Superior Court in each of the 58 counties in California. The number of judges in each Superior Court depends on how much business the court has. The judges in the Superior Courts are elected directly by the people for six years.

Map of California Counties

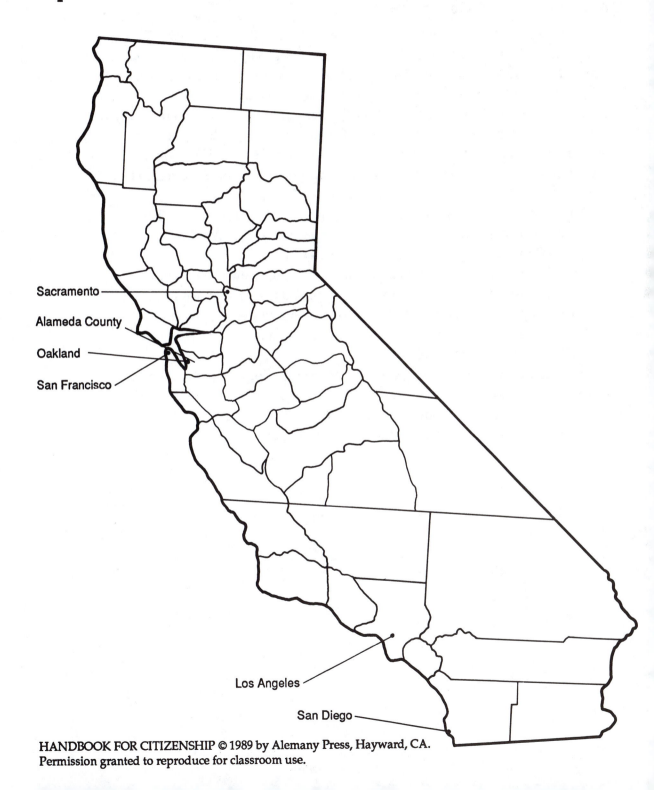

Sacramento
Alameda County
Oakland
San Francisco
Los Angeles
San Diego

Alameda County Government

The Alameda County Charter is the plan of the county government. This government is a republic divided into three parts: legislative, executive, and judicial. The county government meets at the county seat, the city of Oakland.

The Board of Supervisors is the legislative branch of the county government. It makes the laws, called ordinances, for the county. There are five Supervisors in Alameda County. They are elected by the people by districts for four years. The Supervisors decide on the county budget and county services. They oversee tax collection for the county and the cities in the county.

The Board of Supervisors is also part of the executive branch of county government. The Board enforces county ordinances and oversees tax collection for the county and the cities in the county.

The Sheriff works in the executive branch of county government too. He or she is elected by the people for four years and does the police work for the county. The Sheriff works independently, not under the Board of Supervisors. He or she is in charge of the Superior Court and the county jail. There is no one chief executive of Alameda County.

The judicial branch of county government is Superior Court, the state trial court. Superior Court judges are elected by the people for six years. A special kind of court in Superior Court is Juvenile Court for cases about young people under the age of eighteen. The Alameda County Superior Court is in Oakland.

City of Oakland Government
(and other East Bay cities)

The Oakland City Charter gives the plan of government for the city of Oakland. The city government is a republic divided into three parts: legislative, executive, and judicial.

The City Council is the legislative branch. It makes the city laws (ordinances). There are nine members of the Oakland City Council. (All East Bay cities have the same kind of city government, but the number of Council members varies.) The City Council members are elected by the people for four years. One of these nine members is the Mayor. The Mayor presides over the City Council and votes on the ordinances with the Council. The Mayor is the leader of the city and represents the city at ceremonies and business or political meetings, but has no executive powers. The Mayor and the Council members work only part-time.

The City Manager is the chief executive of city government and enforces the laws. The Manager is appointed by the Council and serves according to contract. The Manager is an expert in running city governments and works full time.

The judicial branch of city government is the Municipal Court. Municipal Court is a part of Superior Court serving the city. The judges of Municipal Court are elected by the people for six years. A special kind of court in Municipal Court is Small Claims Court.

Answer Key

Christopher Columbus (p. 21)

B. 1. discovered
2. Spain
3. gold
4. church

C. 1. Italy
2. the king and queen of Spain
3. a new way to India
4. America
5. to find gold and teach the Indians about their church

The First English Settlements (p. 22)

B. 1. Jamestown, Virginia; Plymouth, Massachusetts
2. settlement
3. freedom
4. Pilgrims
5. *Mayflower*
6. colonies

C. 1. Yes.
2. They wanted freedom to work and to make a good life for themselves.
3. winter; The Indians helped them.
4. a piece of land controlled by an <u>outside</u> government; A state has its <u>own</u> government.

Thanksgiving (p. 23)

B. 1. holiday
2. special
3. Pilgrims
4. Indians
5. turkey, corn, pumpkin; cranberries, nuts

C. 1. to give thanks for the good things in life
2. England
3. They wanted freedom of religion.
4. It was winter and they had no food and no houses.

The Growth of the Colonies and Trouble with England (p. 25)

B. 1. Europe
2. England
3. tea
4. protest
5. Boston Tea Party

C. (See map, pp. 6–7)
1. New Hampshire, Massachusetts, Connecticut, Rhode Island, Pennsylvania, New Jersey, New York, Delaware, Maryland, Virginia, North Carolina, South Carolina, Georgia
2. They learned to live and work together.
3. high taxes
4. to hide who they really were
5. a protest against high taxes; Americans dressed up like Indians and threw English tea into Boston harbor.

The Revolutionary War (p. 27)

B. 1. angry
2. arrest
3. harbor
4. Leaders
5. country
6. Revolutionary War
7. George Washington
8. won

C. 1. free, to be your own boss
2. They thought he would close their harbors too.
3. 13
4. the War of Independence

The Declaration of Independence (p. 28)

B. 1. Thomas Jefferson
2. Declaration of Independence
3. July 4, 1776
4. birthday
5. equal
6. rights
7. fought

C. 1. July 4, 1776
2. It is the birthday of the United States.
3. a government where all men were equal and a government that protected their rights to life, liberty, and happiness

The First U.S. Government (p. 29)

B. 1. President, courts, money, power
2. weak
3. Congress
4. national

C. 1. England and Spain could take land away from the Americans.
2. to improve the bad government
3. leaders of the 13 states
4. They wrote a new Constitution.

The Writing of the Constitution (p. 31)

B. 1. Constitution
2. Philadelphia
3. adopted
4. power
5. representatives
6. improvement
7. principles

C. 1. three (3)
2. George Washington
3. the Constitution
4. everybody
5. liberty, equality, and justice
6. the people, the state and national governments; the three parts of government; (the two parts of Congress)

The U.S. Flag and the Pledge of Allegiance (p. 33)

B. 1. 50, 13
2. stars
3. stripes
4. republic
5. republic

C. 1. red, white, and blue
2. the country, the government, and the people of the United States
3. to show respect for the flag and the country

George Washington (p. 35)

B. 1. landowner
    2. commander-in-chief
    3. taught
    4. Constitution
    5. elected
    6. first
    7. terms

C. 1. He learned how to live in the woods, how to fight like the Indians, how to fight like the English, and how to be an elected government representative.
    2. military officers from Germany and France
    3. They had <u>no</u> army, and the English had the best army in the world.

The National Anthem (p. 37)

B. 1. anthem
    2. Francis Scott Key
    3. American; English
    4. arrested
    5. fort
    6. banner
    7. flag

C. 1. "The Star-Spangled Banner"; a flag with twinkling stars on it
    2. England and the United States
    3. Washington, D.C.
    4. at night
    5. the United States; ". . . our flag was still there."
    6. He loved it very much.

Abraham Lincoln and the Civil War (p. 39)

B. 1. honest
    2. debates
    3. wrong
    4. President
    5. Civil War
    6. North
    7. North
    8. slaves
    9. Union

C. 1. He taught himself.
    2. He believed that <u>all</u> men, including Black men, were equal and should have the rights in the Constitution.
    3. honest, friendly, kind, helpful
    4. He freed the slaves and saved the Union.

The Constitution (p. 43)

B. 1. Constitution
    2. republic
    3. people
    4. three (3)
    5. amendment
    6. legislative
    7. enforces
    8. judicial

C. 1. a republic
    2. to divide government power; to keep the power in the hands of the people
    3. by amendment
    4. never

The Bill of Rights (p. 45)

B. 1. Bill of Rights
    2. rights, freedoms
    3. freedom
    4. speech
    5. press
    6. religion
    7. jury
    8. people, states

C. 1. to help guarantee their freedom
    2. • freedom of speech,
       • freedom of the press,
       • freedom of religion,
       • freedom to hold meetings,
       • freedom to complain to the government,
       • freedom to be safe in your home,
       • the right to a jury trial,
       • the rights and powers not in the Constitution belong to the people and the states.
    3. no. They are also for non-citizens.
    4. 27

The Amendments (p. 47)

B. 1. Nineteen (19)
    2. Twenty-Six (26)
    3. Fifteen (15)
    4. Twenty-Two (22)
    5. Sixteen (16)
    6. Fourteen (14)

C. 1. President and Vice-President
    2. by the 13th Amendment
    3. the 24th Amendment
    4. by the people (17th Amendment)
    5. the 18th; by the 21st ; the majority of the people did not agree with it.
    6. indirectly by the people (12th Amendment)
    7. the Vice-President; the 25th Amendment
    8. appointed by the President with consent of the Congress; the 25th Amendment

The Federal Government (p. 48)

B. 1. people
    2. democracy
    3. republic
    4. federal
    5. representatives
    6. majority

C. 1. through voting, by winning a majority of votes
    2. so that the government will continue to be a government of all the people
    3. The Constitution divides the government into three parts. The Bill of Rights gives many rights to the people. It also gives the powers not in the Constitution to the people.

Other Governments: Dictatorships (p. 49)

B. 1. dictatorship
   2. Communism
   3. communism; dictatorships

C. 1. no
   2. They want to be free to control their government and their lives.
   3. no!

Washington, D.C. (p. 50)

B. 1. Washington, D.C.
   2. eastern
   3. parts; branches, departments
   4. White House
   5. Capitol
   6. check up

C. 1. District of Columbia
   2. Three; legislative, executive, judicial
   3. legislative—makes laws
      executive—enforces laws
      judicial—explains laws
   4. makes laws; enforces laws
   5. in the Supreme Court Building; explain laws

Legislative Branch (p. 53)

B. 1. legislative
   2. two
   3. Senate
   4. House of Representatives
   5. people
   6. Six (6); two (2)
   7. Speaker
   8. state

C. 1. Congress
   2. Senate; House of Representatives
   3. It depends on the population of the state.
   4. in the Capitol building
   5. A bill must pass both houses of Congress by a majority vote and be signed by the President.
   6. more than half (1/2); at least two-thirds (2/3)
   7. _____ (See Government Officers chart on p. 61)
   8. _____ (See p. 61)
   9. President pro tempore of the Senate
   10. to make laws,
       to declare war,
       to provide money for the military, post offices and U.S. courts,
       to coin money,
       to pass laws to borrow money, for Washington, D.C., naturalization, and to carry out powers, and so on. (See p. 52)
   11. to vote on the President's appointments to the cabinet and the federal courts,
       to vote on treaties signed by the President,
       to hold impeachment trials,
       to vote for a Vice-President when necessary
   12. to begin a law to raise money,
       to bring a bill of impeachment,
       to vote for a President when necessary
   13. spend money except by law,
       take away the right of *habeas corpus*,
       tax exports

Executive Branch (p. 55)

B. 1. executive
   2. President
   3. Vice-President; Cabinet
   4. native-born
   5. four
   6. two
   7. people

C. 1. the President
   2. the Vice-President
   3. He or she must be a native-born citizen, 35 years old, have lived in the United States 14 years before becoming President.
   4. the Constitution
   5. to protect and follow the Constitution
   6. to enforce laws,
      to sign and veto bills,
      to be commander-in-chief of the military,
      to appoint Cabinet officers, U.S. judges, and sign treaties with consent of the Senate, and so on. (See p. 54)
   7. the Congress (controls money)
      the Senate (consents to appointments)
      the people (election), and so on.
   8. (See your state in the Appendices, pp. 74–82)
   9. in the White House in Washington, D.C.
  10. ———, ———
  11. elected indirectly by the people

The Cabinet (p. 57)

B. 1. 14
   2. the Interior
   3. Attorney General
   4. State
   5. Treasury
   6. Commerce
   7. Labor
   8. Attorney General
   9. Education
  10. Energy
  11. President
  12. Defense
  13. Senate

C. 1. a group of 14 people that helps the President enforce the laws
   2. _____ (See p. 61)
   3. at the President's pleasure
   4. _____ (See p. 61)

Judicial Branch (p. 59)

B. 1. nine (9)
   2. District Court
   3. U.S. Supreme Court
   4. explains
   5. federal
   6. Washington, D.C.
   7. Senate
   8. Congress
   9. Chief Justice

C. 1. the Constitution
   2. for life
   3. one (1); 11; 91
   4. one (1)
   5. ——— (See p. 61)
   6. the U.S. Supreme Court
   7. the U.S. Supreme Court

State Government (p. 65)

B. 1. states
2. lakes, rivers
3. naturalization
4. influenced
5. union
6. education
7. mountains

C. 1. ____ (See map pp. 6–7)
2. ____
3. ____
4. ____
5. ____ (See Appendices, pp. 74–82)
6. ____ (See Appendices, pp. 74–82)
7. ____ (See Appendices, pp. 74–82)
8. ____ (See p. 71)
9. ____ (See p. 71)

County Government (p. 67)

B. 1. Sheriff
2. Charter
3. Local
4. provide (distribute, contribute)
5. collects
6. fees
7. libraries
8. property

C. 1. They take care of needs the bigger governments cannot handle.
2. ____ (See p. 71)
3. ____ (See p. 71)
4. ____ (See p. 71)

5. enforce state laws in local areas,
   distribute federal and state
      money to the poor and disabled,
   contribute to local schools,
   take care of county roads, parks and
      lands,
   provide health care for the poor,
      and so on.
   (See p. 66 under <u>Services</u>)

City Government (p. 69)

B. 1. municipal
2. Mayor
3. Mayor
4. Manager
5. Council
6. Mayor

C. 1. provide police, fire and emergency
      protection,
   keep the city clean,
   take care of city property,
      streets and parks, and so on.
   (See p. 68 under <u>Services</u>)
2. from federal and state governments,
   from the county where
      they are located,
   from city fees and fines
3. _____
4. _____
5. ____ (See p. 71)
6. ____ (See p. 71)
7. ____ (See p. 71)

Practice Questions and Answers: Cassette Tape/Tapescript

How to Use the Tape and Tapescript

Handbook for Citizenship has provided you with the information you need to answer the questions on the oral naturalization exam. It is helpful to practice oral use of this information before taking the test. A cassette tape containing **Practice Questions and Answers** is available separately from Alemany Press. The following pages, 98–103, are designed as a **tapescript** for you to follow when listening and responding to the Practice Questions on the tape. If you don't have the tape, your teacher or another person can read the questions from the tapescript and you can practice listening and answering.

First, listen to each question and then answer out loud from memory without looking at the tapescript (and before listening to the recorded answer, if you are using the tape). If you cannot answer some of the questions, review the information on your petition forms. Also review the chapters on United States History, and United States, State, and Local Government and other information you have collected about your state's history and government. **Next,** listen to the questions once with your book open, looking at the questions with the answers covered while you respond. **Finally,** if necessary, listen and respond to the questions again while looking at both the questions and the answers on the script.

Your goal in these practice steps is to learn how to listen and respond to the questions with the book closed. *The best practice is without the script!*

The tapescript on the following pages contains both the instructions to you and the Practice Questions and Answers *exactly as recorded on the cassette tape.* Apart from the instructions, the tape and tapescript consist of three parts that reflect the primary areas of focus on the oral naturalization exam:

Part 1) Questions About Information on the United States Naturalization Petition Forms,

Part 2) Questions About United States History and Government, and

Part 3) The Most Commonly Asked Questions.

In these three parts, certain answers are not given where you are expected to provide specific information about yourself, your state, county, city, or the names of government officers. **In some instances,** *only on the tapescript,* **recommended answers or additional information appear in parentheses ( ).**

Short answers that are not complete sentences are expected and accepted by INS examiners. However, complete sentences are sometimes used on the tape and tapescript to provide natural-sounding language. **When complete sentences are used,** *the key information in each sentence is underlined on the* **tapescript.**

Tapescript, Part 1 (side 1)

Questions About Information on the United States Naturalization Petition Forms

Listen carefully to each question. It will not be repeated. After each question, stop the tape and answer the question out loud. No recorded answers will be given for this section of the tape, because you must respond correctly, using the personal information you have written on your petition forms. Let's begin:

1. Do you swear that all your statements are true and correct?

    1. (Yes.)

2. Where were you born?

    2. (place)

3. When were you born?

    3. (month, day, year)

4. Do you intend to live in the United States?

    4. (Yes.)

5. Do you owe any Federal income tax?

    5. (No.)

6. Have you ever been arrested?

    6.

7. Have you ever committed a crime?

    7.

8. Do you believe in the United States Constitution?

    8. (Yes.)

9. How many times have you been married?

    9.

10. Are you willing to take the full oath of allegiance to the United States?

    10.

11. How many children do you have?

    11.

12. Do you receive welfare or money from the government?

    12.

13. Have you been out of the United States since you arrived?

    13.

14. When were you lawfully admitted for permanent residence?

    14.

15. Can you speak, read, and write English?

    15. (Yes.)

16. Why do you want to be a United States citizen?

    16.

This is the end of Part 1.

Tapescript, Part 2 (side 1)

Questions About United States History and Government

Listen carefully to each question. It will not be repeated. After each question, stop the tape and answer the question out loud. Then turn on the tape recorder again to check your answer. No answers will be given for questions 8, 15, and 16. Let's begin:

1. Who is the chief executive of the United States?
2. How is the chief executive elected?

3. Who is the head of the Naturalization Service?

4. What is a republic?

5. What are the qualifications for President?

6. How many original states were there?
7. How do cabinet officers get their positions?
8. Who is the Chief Justice of the United States Supreme Court?
9. Why do we have three branches of government?
10. How long do United States Senators serve?
11. How long do United States Representatives serve?
12. What is the Twenty-Sixth Amendment?

1. <u>The President</u>; you may also give the President's name.
2. He or she is <u>elected indirectly by the people.</u>
3. <u>The United States Attorney General</u>; you may also give the Attorney General's name.
4. It is <u>a government elected by the people.</u>
5. To be President a person must:
   be <u>a native-born citizen,</u>
   be at least <u>35 years old,</u> and
   have <u>lived in the United States 14 years</u> before election.
6. 13
7. They are <u>appointed by the President with consent of the Senate.</u>
8. (Give the name.)

9. <u>Three branches</u> of government <u>divide government power.</u>

10. six years

11. two years

12. It gives 18-year-olds the right to vote.

(continued)

Questions About United States History and Government, (continued)

13. What is the First Amendment?

13. It gives <u>freedom of speech</u>, <u>freedom of press</u>, <u>freedom of religion</u>, <u>freedom to hold meetings</u>, and <u>freedom to complain to the government</u>.

14. What is the Nineteenth Amendment?

14. It gives women the right to vote.

15. When did your state become a state?

15. (Give the date.)

16. How many electoral votes does your state have for President?

16. (Give the number.)

17. What are the principles of the Constitution?

17. liberty, equality, and justice

18. Who were the first three Presidents?

18. George Washington, John Adams, and Thomas Jefferson

19. What were the last two states to become states?

19. Alaska and Hawaii

20. Which Presidents were assassinated (killed) in office?

20. Abraham Lincoln, James Garfield, William McKinley, and John F. Kennedy

This is the end of Part 2. Fast forward to the end of the tape. Then turn it over and listen to Part 3.

Tapescript, Part 3 (side 2)

The Most Commonly Asked Questions

Listen carefully to each question. It will not be repeated. After each question, stop the tape and answer the question out loud. Then turn on the tape recorder again to check your answer. No answers will be given for questions 2, 10, 13, 29 through 35, 37 and 38. Let's begin:

1. Who was the first President?

1. George Washington

2. Who are the President and Vice-President now?

2. (Give the names.)

3. What is the Constitution?

3. It is <u>the highest law of the United States</u>.

4. How many amendments are there to the United States Constitution?

4. **27**

5. How many parts are there in the government?

5. three

6. Name the parts of the government.

6. the <u>legislative</u> part, the <u>executive</u> part, and the <u>judicial</u> part

7. What does each part of government do?

7. The legislative part <u>makes laws</u>. The executive part <u>enforces laws</u>. The judicial part <u>explains laws</u>.

8. How many United States Senators are there?

8. 100

9. How many United States Senators does each state have?

9. two

10. Who are the United States Senators from your state?

10. (Give the names.)

11. How many United States Representatives are there?

11. 435

12. How many United States Representatives does each state have?

12. The number of United States representatives from each state <u>depends on the population</u> of the state.

13. How many United States Representatives does your state have?

13. (Give the number.)

14. What is the Bill of Rights?

14. It is the <u>first ten amendments</u> to the Constitution.

(continued)

The Most Commonly Asked Questions (continued)

15. Name some of the rights in the Bill of Rights.

15. Some of the rights are:
    <u>freedom of speech</u>,
    <u>freedom of press</u>,
    <u>freedom of religion</u>,
    <u>freedom to hold meetings</u>,
    <u>freedom to be safe at home</u>,
    <u>freedom to complain to the government</u>, and
    <u>the right to a jury trial</u>.
    All rights and powers not in the Constitution belong to the people and the states.

16. Why is the Declaration of Independence important?

16. It is the beginning of the United States.

17. When was the Declaration of Independence signed?

17. July 4, 1776

18. Who was Abraham Lincoln?

18. He was the 16th <u>President</u>. <u>He served during the Civil War</u>.

19. What did Abraham Lincoln do?

19. He freed the slaves and saved the Union.

20. What is the capital of the United States?

20. Washington, D.C.

21. What is the highest United States court called?

21. the United States <u>Supreme Court</u>

22. How many judges sit on the United States Supreme Court?

22. nine

23. Can you become President? Why?

23. No. I am <u>not a native-born</u> United States <u>citizen</u>.

24. What is the Cabinet?

24. It is <u>a group of 14 people who help the President</u> enforce the laws.

25. Who makes United States laws?

25. Congress

26. How many parts does Congress have?

26. two

27. What are the parts of Congress called?

27. the Senate and the House of Representatives

(continued)

The Most Commonly Asked Questions (continued)

28. What form or what kind of government does the United States have?

28. The United States government is <u>a republic</u> or a democracy.

29. Are you a Communist? Do you believe in communism?

29. (No.) (No.)

30. Are you willing to bear arms for the United States?

30.

31. What is the capital of your state?

31.

32. Who makes the laws for your state?

32.

33. How many parts are there in the legislative branch of your state government?

33.

34. What are the parts of the legislative branch of your state government called?

34.

35. Who is the Governor of your state?

35.

36. What is the Governor's job?

36. to enforce the laws of the state

37. Who makes the laws for your county?

37.

38. Who makes the laws for your city?

38.

39. What are the colors in the United States flag?

39. red, white, and blue

40. How many stars and stripes does the United States flag have?

40. The flag has <u>50 stars</u> (for the present 50 states) and <u>13 stripes</u> (for the original 13 states).

This is the end of Part 3 and the Practice Questions and Answers tape.

Writing Practice for the Naturalization Exam

Sample Sentences

At the end of the naturalization exam the applicant for citizenship will be asked to write a simple English sentence. The examiner will tell the applicant what to write. The following sample sentences have been taken from past exams. Practice writing the sentences. Fill in the blanks and be sure to spell the words correctly.

1. There are _____ children in my family.
   (number)

2. My children go to school.

3. They are learning English.

4. My house is in the city.

5. I live in _____ .
   (your city and state)

6. I take the bus to work.

7. I work in a _____ .
   (place where you work)

8. I am _____ .
   (your job)

9. I want to be a citizen of the United States.

10. I will be a good citizen.

11. I believe in the Constitution.

12. All men are free.

13. I was born in _____ .
    (your country)

14. My family is happy to be in America.

15. I was married in _____ .
    (year)

16. I study citizenship at adult school.

17. The woman eats in a restaurant.

18. The man has a good job.

19. My shirt is white.

20. I can speak English.